MELVILLE'S POETRY:
Toward the Enlarged Heart

MELVILLE'S POETRY:
Toward the Enlarged Heart

A THEMATIC STUDY
OF THREE IGNORED MAJOR POEMS

Aaron Kramer

Rutherford • *Madison* • *Teaneck*
FAIRLEIGH DICKINSON UNIVERSITY PRESS

Associated University Presses, Inc.
Cranbury, New Jersey 08512

ISBN: 0-8386-1002-1
Printed in the United States of America

CONTENTS

Introductory Essay   9
Bridegroom Dick   49
The Scout Toward Aldie   64
Marquis de Grandvin   90
Notes   138
Selected Bibliography   145

MELVILLE'S POETRY:
Toward the Enlarged Heart

INTRODUCTORY ESSAY

Even if a critic as sober as Randall Jarrell[1] had not ranked Whitman, Dickinson, and Melville as America's best 19th-century poets, one might have expected that by now Melville's poetry would have received at least a preliminary exploration. Out of sheer curiosity, if not for purposes of creative scholarship, every production of his final 35 years should have been examined for any illuminations it might offer of his philosophic, emotional, and artistic development after 1856, and for any new light it might throw on those few towering works of fiction which are milked dry year after year in lectures, essays, and dissertations.

Yet the bulk of Melville's poetic output is either altogether ignored by Melville specialists in their most ambitious commentaries, or apologized for in one or two condescending phrases based less on a study of the poems than on an inherited attitude.

In recent years, however, a few inroads have been made. The Civil War group, *Clarel,* and certain of the later pieces have received some discussion, and a slightly varying cluster of excerpts is now available in anthologies and selected editions.

In the hope of expanding the area of study and appreciation, I am here focusing on several key poems which have never been chosen for reprint aside from collected editions, and which have had little or no critical attention.[2] If nothing more, I hope to demonstrate that Mel-

ville's unread poems contain important values, that a
number of major themes emerge, that the great shift
from the despair of *The Confidence Man* to the affirma-
tion of *Billy Budd* is dramatically prepared for in some
of these poems.

A case in point is "Bridegroom Dick." Among the
longest of Melville's poems published during his lifetime,
it occupies more than two-fifths of the 1888 volume,
John Marr and Other Sailors. Yet it has gone generally
undiscussed,[3] and in almost fifty years has seldom been
reprinted. Howard P. Vincent, in a footnote to the
Collected Poems, dismisses it as a companion-piece to
White-Jacket. Hennig Cohen's edition of *Battle-Pieces,*
and Robert Penn Warren's *Selected Poems of Herman
Melville,* annotate the poem richly, but fail to evaluate it.

It is true, as Vincent points out, that the poem shares
with *White-Jacket* several characters and incidents based
on Melville's own experiences aboard the *United States,*
and that the giant Finn of the poem "is derived from
Melville's memory of the flogging of William Hoff . . .
for disrespectful conduct to his superiors."[4] The climax
of "Bridegroom Dick," however, is the culprit's *failure*
to be flogged; that fact alone should alert the reader to
the poem's significance as an expression of Melville's
dominant attitudes in his final years.

In the novel there are two instances where floggings
are bypassed, but these are many-times-outweighed by
the long, vivid chapters narrating punishments brutally
and unjustly inflicted. Captain Claret, responsible for
those harsh acts and for such other cruelties as the
head-bumping "games" imposed on two blacks, is trans-
formed to an amazing degree in the poem, where "under
starred bunting" Captain Turret looms "gigantic" with
his "florid full face and fine silvered hair." The change
in his name could not be more apt. The Claret of *White-
Jacket* "continually kept himself in an uncertain equi-

librio between soberness and its reverse; which equilibrio might be destroyed by the first sharp vicissitude of events." Turret, in the poem, truly towers above the situation in which he finds himself. The fact that he "the brave wine could stow" is to his credit here, a symbol of the large-heartedness celebrated in the poem.

In the novel Melville characterizes at length those in the lower echelons of command, whose self-serving and malicious proclivities thrive freely in the world of the *Neversink*. He discusses in detail "the unscrupulous cupidity" of many pursers on American warships, and deals even more fully with the chaplain, a "transcendental divine" whose abstruse, learned sermons "never, in the remotest manner, attacked the everyday vices of the 19th century, as eminently illustrated in our man-of-war world." But he reserves his fury for the man-killing ship-surgeon, a savage portrayal that extends through three chapters (61-63) and is as harrowing as anything in Sinclair's *The Jungle*.

These personages have not changed in the poem; but their function is radically altered. The chaplain is presented not directly, but in contrast to the admirable Tom Light:

> Tom was a man
> In contrast queer with Chaplain Le Fan,
> Who blessed us at morn, and at night yet again,
> D---ning us only in decorous strain;
> Preaching 'tween the guns—each cutlass in its place—
> From text that averred old Adam a hard case . . .
> O Tom, but he knew a blue-jacket's ways . . .
> Only a sailor sailors heartily praise.
>
> *(228-42)*

Similarly, the surgeon is demoted to the role of foil for the vibrant Finn who is awaiting punishment:

Never venturing a caveat whatever may betide,
Though functionally here on humanity's side,
The grave Surgeon shows, like the formal physician
Attending the rack o' the Spanish Inquisition.
                                                (291-94)

And the purser dwindles to "fat Purser Smart," past
whom Captain Turret brushes with generous gesture
and speech.

It is not surprising, consistent with the above shifts in
emphasis, that Melville reduces the heart-chilling Arti-
cles of War—so extensively quoted, explained, and criti-
cized in *White-Jacket* (Chapters 70, 71, 72, 74, and
88)—to a mere feint in the poem:

Now the culprit he liked . . .
But what of that now? In the martinet-mien
Read the *Articles of War,* heed the naval routine . . .
                                                (301-06)

Clearly the iniquities of naval life which had hit young
Melville with tremendous impact in 1843 and which he
felt impelled to expose in *White-Jacket* seven years
later, were no longer uppermost in his mind when he
came to write "Bridegroom Dick." To suggest that his
memory was by now befogged would hardly do. He
need merely have skimmed through the pages of *White-
Jacket* to recall the past; and his sharp, if brief, charac-
terizations of chaplain, purser, and surgeon are sufficient
evidence of how well that voyage was remembered.

A more plausible explanation would be that Melville
is speaking not directly, as in the early novel, of a cap-
tain who (in Chapter 67) drove the youthful tar to the
edge of murder and suicide, but indirectly, through a
persona, a long-retired and lonely salt in whose nostalgic
imagination the perished time was tinged with gold. Like
the better-known sea-poems—"John Marr," "Tom Dead-
light," "Jack Roy," and "To Ned"—this poem is elegiac;

the old wounds have long since healed. Thus, what was once terrifying and overwhelming becomes in retrospect an organic element of life, to be anatomized and outmatched; what was good then is now raised to mythic proportions.

One cannot automatically equate this fine Browning-esque soliloquy with the poet's own mood at the time of writing; but there is a strong likelihood that here, as in many other late pieces, Melville has merely managed "to slip on" what Jay Leyda calls "a robe of objectivity"[5] before allowing his feelings to be published.

A dozen years earlier, in Clarel's robe, he had thoroughly considered and ultimately rejected despair in favor of what James E. Miller terms "the brotherhood of humanity."[6] A superb epilogue had urged the hero to keep his heart and concentrate on "the issues there." Bridegroom Dick has learned that lesson long before we hear his soliloquy, and his portrayal of the shipboard life is softened by his personal good nature. Whether the poem suffers in depth, complexity, and dramatic power as a result is another matter; but it surely represents a large step away from the *White-Jacket* world, dominated by men like Claggart, toward the world of *Billy Budd*, in which good triumphs.

Tyrus Hillway[7] suggests that recent Melville critics, in selecting favorite poems, "betray a preference for those denoting an attitude of pessimism." This undoubtedly helps explain the shoddy treatment given to poems like "Bridegroom Dick." But Hillway's own characterization of the piece as "a lament for old seamen" is somewhat misleading, for—while recommending it—he ignores the rich prophetic materials contained within its elegiac framework.

It is necessary, at the outset, to stress that the passages of nostalgia in "Bridegroom Dick" almost invariably imply a condemnation of the current era; in glorifying a noble past he performs the prophet's mission of juxta-

posing it against an ignoble present. Early in the poem
he apostrophizes an old-style vessel, "veteran o' the Heart-
o'-Oak war" (reminiscent of the song in *White-Jacket:*
"Hearts of oak are our ships") :

> Never on *you* did the iron-clads jar!
> Your open deck when the boarder assailed,
> The frank old heroic hand-to-hand then availed.
>
> *(79-81)*

This tribute to "the Old Order," a vanished time of
openness, courage, and grace, prepares us for the cul-
minating passage many pages later; it is not so much
that the sailors, those "pennoned fine fellows," are re-
tired or dead, but that "tradition was lost and we learned
strange ways." Melville beweeps Genteel Jack's "watch-
chain with love's jeweled tokens abounding . . ." be-
cause it is out of place in "a lack-lustre day," a time of
functionalism. America has turned into a nation of black-
smiths who "Into smithereens smite the solid old re-
nown." Typical of his dramatic bent, the poet satirizes
his materialistic epoch by making its hammers speak
"with a *rat-tat-tat*":

> Handier a *derby* than a lacked cocked hat!
> The *Monitor* was ugly, but she served us right well,
> Better than the *Cumberland,* a beauty and a belle.
>
> *(405-07)*

He sees something morally symptomatic in designing
ships of "impenetrable armor—all-perforating shot,"
that sneakily deal "under the waterline . . . a *ram's*
blow":

> And foul fall the knuckles that strike below the belt.
> Nor brave the inventions that serve to replace
> The openness of valor while dismantling the grace.
>
> *(415-17)*

It is appropriate for the sailor and the writer, both sunken into obscurity, each with an audience of one, to end on a note of militant nostalgia. The ugly present is transitory; what is noble remains "moored in the roadstead of fame . . . / Their long shadows dwarf us, their flags are as flame . . ."

Had Hennig Cohen[8] considered the strength of this protest, and the poet's habit of letting what he despises speak in its own voice (as far back as the songs of war and gold-rush, in *Mardi*), he might have interpreted differently those Civil War poems, "The Temeraire" and "A Utilitarian View of the Monitor's Fight." For the first is a delicately wrought Melville dirge, while the second matches the hardness of the speaker with the hardest form Melville can accomplish. Cohen's praise of that form for its lack "of a false rhetoric" seems to reflect his own preferences in modern poetry rather than a recognition of the disgust behind Melville's stylistic strategy.

For Melville, as we shall see, returns to this theme throughout his poetic career—lamenting the Old Order with a romantic rhetoric that for him rings true, while depicting the utilitarian New Order with the harshest words he can muster.

A second major theme of "Bridegroom Dick," as of *Clarel* and *Billy Budd,* is the superiority of heart over *really* head, instinct over strategy, naturalness over formalism, spontaneity over prudence. (This is, of course, linked with his loyalty to a past which has been vanquished by a cold, arrogant, and pragmatically motivated intellectualism.) The opposed ways of life are almost invariably juxtaposed, beginning with the self-portrait that introduces the theme:

Chirrupy even when crosses rubbed me . . .
Pleasant at a yarn, Bob O'Linkum in a song . . .

To me would the officers say a word cheery—
Break through the starch o' the quarter-deck realm . . .
Bored nigh to death with the navy etiquette,
Yearning, too, for fun, some younker, a cadet . . .
Boy-like would unbend to Bridegroom Dick.
But a limit there was—a check, d'ye see:
Those fine young aristocrats knew their degree.
                                                    (16–41)

The bleak Chaplain Le Fan, Calvinistically damning
"in decorous strain" the sailors he didn't really know,
is compared with Tom Tight, liked by the sailors even
when he scolded them, because "he knew a blue-jacket's
ways . . . / Only a sailor sailors heartily praise." Such
heartless personages as "the blue-nosed boatswain," his
aides eager to be handed the thongs, and the surgeon
who never protests that a man is being flogged too hard,
are introduced right after a vivid description of the
magnificent Finn who awaits his flogging:

Our three-decker's giant, a grand boatswain's mate,
Manliest of men in his own natural senses;
But driven stark mad by the devil's drugged stuff,
Storming all aboard from his run-ashore late,
Challenging to battle, vouchsafing no pretenses,
A reeling King Ogg, delirious in power,
The quarter-deck carronades he seemed to make cower.
"Put him in *brig* there!" said Lieutenant Marrot.
"Put him in *brig!*" back he mocked like a parrot;
"Try it, then!" swaying a fist like Thor's sledge,
And making the pigmy constables hedge . . .
                                                    (256–66)

At this point, by the undiminished power of his fictive
imagination and ethical vision, Melville transforms an
actually administered flogging into one which is rejected
by "a tall captain" who can appreciate "a Titan subordi-

nate and true *sailor-man* . . ." Thus, the central event
of "Bridegroom Dick," which in *White-Jacket* would
have been a bitter lesson to a natural man of how he
must behave in order to survive on a warship, becomes
instead a lesson in manliness and Christian justice to
those thwarted instruments of Articles of War justice—
the boatswain "complexioned like slag," his bloodthirsty
assistants, the Inquisitional Surgeon, and:

> . . . that sore one, crabbed and severe,
> Lieutenant Don Lumbago, an arch scrutineer . . .
> Testy as touchwood, to pry and to peer.
> *(333-38)*

With a dramatic sense and didactic motive reminiscent
of Shakespeare's best rulers, Capt. Turret "in the mar-
tinet-mien" reads the Articles of War, has the Finn tied
up, stripped to the waist, weeping with shame. At this
moment he cries:

> Untie him—so!
> Submission is enough, Man, you may go . . .
> Flog? Never meant it—hadn't any heart.
> Degrade that tall fellow?
> *(324-28)*

The Captain has acted in accordance with the epilogue
of *Clarel,* has truly minded "the issues" in his heart, has
inspiringly grown—along with both Captain Vere and
Billy Budd—into what Warner Berthoff calls "the con-
dition of magnanimity."[9]
  It may not be altogether far-fetched to link this ex-
traordinary moment ("Submission is enough") with the
problem of Northern justice toward the defeated South,
especially as treated in the penultimate poem of *Battle-
Pieces,* "Lee in the Capitol," and the urgent prose sup-
plement which follows. Called before the Senate, Lee
declares:

> Push not your triumph; do not urge
> Submissiveness beyond the verge . . .
> To elect in magnanimity is wise . . .
> What sounder fruit than re-established law?

As the Finn in "Bridegroom Dick" towers above his judges, so does "Intrepid" Lee loom gigantic beside the Northern senators, accepting his doom (not in accordance with fact, but through the poetic license of Melville, who—to quote Richard H. Fogle[10]—rounded out "the imperfections of history," transforming "fact to luminous meaning"). Fogle rightly points out that the argument of Lee is as Machiavellian as it is Christian—stressing political wisdom—and this emphasis in 1865 serves as a significant gauge for Melville's shift in the '70s and '80s; but the theme of forgiveness and reconciliation recurs in others of the *Battle-Pieces:* "Man honors man . . . Brave one! I here implore your hand . . ." ("Magnanimity Baffled"); "Perish their Cause! but mark the men . . . Spare Spleen her ire . . ." ("Rebel Color-Bearers at Shiloh"); "Who joys at her [Charleston's] wild despairing . . . Christ, the Forgiver, convert his mind" ("The Swamp Angel").

What makes the parallel seem especially pertinent is a remarkable return to the Civil War in "Bridegroom Dick"—23 years after Appomattox. The old sailor is still haunted by "The troublous colic o' intestine war." Discussing the Battle for the Bay, he emphasizes that he "joys in the man nor brags about the race." As in *Battle-Pieces,* he expresses outrage at "Our flag blown to shreds . . . in Secession's foul weather," but refuses to condemn the individual Confederate fighter:

> Duty? It pulled with more than one string . . .
> The flag and your kin, how be true unto both?
> If one plight ye keep, then ye break the other troth.
> *(119–22)*

Unexpectedly, the fateful and nightmarish quality of
that war—"the hurricane unchained"—flickers up from
the lines of "Bridegroom Dick":

> And partners were taken, and the red dance began,
> War's red dance o' death!
>
> (*111-12*)

In the course of recalling that conflict, the protagonist
briefly but cogently introduces two themes which are
expanded in other Melville works. The first is a por-
trayal of wickedness—American in this case—the wick-
edness of those who see war only in terms of personal
profit:

> Of all these thrills thrilled at keelson, and throes,
> Little felt the shoddyites a-toasting o' their toes;
> In mart and bazaar Lucre chuckled the huzza,
> Coining the dollars in the bloody mint of war.
>
> (*125-28*)

The second is a bitter characterization of the universe
and the forces controlling it, so reminiscent of Glouces-
ter's "As flies to wanton boys, are we to the gods; / They
kill us for their sport":

> A humming-top, ay, for the little boy-gods
> Flogging it well with their smart little rods,
> Tittering at time and the coil uncurled.
>
> (*172-74*)

Bridegroom Dick apologizes gracefully to his wife for
this grim evaluation of reality:

> But sour if I get, giving truth her due,
> Honey-sweet forever, wife, will Dick be to *you!*
>
> (*177-78*)

The second line supports Leon Howard's view of the
poem as an expression of Melville's "increased devotion

to Lizzie"[11] after their son's death in 1886; the first line, however, must be read as one more enunciation of the prophet's role which Melville had been performing and defining—with increased doggedness—throughout his career. That his persona, *and* his crucial parenthetical couplet, achieved a balance of sour and sweet, is symbolic of the poet's lifelong goal and ultimate triumph.

Many of the other generally ignored poems demonstrate, as does "Bridegroom Dick," the unslackened vigor of Melville's ethical concern. To read them without condescension is to discover that the "thirty year interval"[12] between *The Confidence Man* and *Billy Budd,* which so impresses Berthoff, was no interval at all.

Among the *Battle-Pieces,* "The Scout Toward Aldie" has suffered a more unwarranted neglect than any other poem. It has generally gone unmentioned by those who discuss Melville's position on the Civil War. Montague, however, in "Melville's *Battle-Pieces,*" conveniently dismisses it in two words: "long, prolix."[13] The only critics who have obviously given serious attention to this extraordinary 800-line ballad are Leon Howard and Richard H. Fogle. Once again, Hennig Cohen and Robert Penn Warren provide fine annotations, but avoid discussing the poem.

Howard's approach[14] is biographical; he is interested in the poem mostly because it deals with an important Melville event: "the last active adventure of his life." But in an acute reading Howard finds that the actual episode—accompanying a scouting party into Virginia partisan country—was less important "than the emotional attitude . . . which later enabled him to transform 'what might have been' into a narrative that seemed more real than the historical occurrences." Howard rightly speaks of it as "the most ambitious of his

Civil War poems," without, however, indicating the riches it offers.

Fogle,[15] on the other hand, focuses squarely on the poem, and produces the only creative comment it has as yet received. While praising its "vigorous narrative, sardonic humor, and vividly realistic description," and noting that it "catches the spirit of the Border ballad," he concludes that "the poem does not quite manage to stand on its own feet." The defect, as he sees it, is its "too heavy" emphasis on the Rebel guerrilla leader, John Mosby, whose name occurs near the close of each stanza. But he adds that this very defect "is interesting and characteristic, for Mosby becomes an omnipresent principle of hidden danger and evil . . . like the gliding shark . . ."

I believe that Fogle has seriously misread the poem by approaching it overprepared. What he considers its defect is in fact its strength, both stylistically and ethically. It is easy to see how a reader too-well-acquainted with Melville's recurrent symbols might be misled, for as early as the second stanza Mosby rides through the forest "As glides in seas the shark." This simile is bolstered throughout the opening pages by such ominous phrases as: "Of Mosby best beware . . . Mosby's men fell deeds can do . . . Mosby sallied late, brave blood to spill . . . Fit land for Mosby or for crime . . ." His men "dare to prowl" in sight of the Capitol Dome; and a member of the scouting party, recalling a Northern soldier shot while drinking from a brook, blames Mosby for thinking that "in war all's fair." This, however, represents not Melville's attitude toward the guerrilla chieftain but the motivation of the young Colonel and his scouting party. Even at the beginning the evidence is building that "the moment of truth" in the woods toward which the vainglorious Colonel moves is against a bold and dynamic foe whose "lads" often "enlarge" their hearts "In revelry by some gorge's marge."

Midway, even before the confrontation begins, Mosby —largely by the constant reminder of his name and of his genius for ambush—has achieved for the reader the rank of mythic hero, and the portrait of his followers in captivity dramatically shifts our sympathy toward them. The Northerner shot while drinking at a brook is counterbalanced by the Southerner, a middle-aged father, who remarks: "They shot at my heart when my hands were up." When a young rebel is offered whiskey he replies:

> ". . . any guile?
> For if you think we'll blab—why, then
> You don't know Mosby or his men."
>
> *(376-78)*

The description of these Confederates (as in "The Released Rebel Prisoner," "The Rebel Color-Bearers at Shiloh," and other Civil War poems) is loving and generous:

> Virginians; some of family-pride,
> And young, and full of fire, and fine
>   In open feature and cheek that glowed;
>   And here thralled vagabonds now they ride . . .
>
> *(332-35)*

This sympathy, later to be enunciated in "Bridegroom Dick," is far more remarkable for a Northern poet addressing a hate-wracked Northern audience soon after accompanying a Northern force and immediately after his own cousin, Col. Gansevoort, has captured Mosby's camp. Around the campfire young prisoners sing:

> I'm for the South! says the leafage green . . .
> . . . bluebirds! keep away, and fear
> The ambuscade in bushes here.
>
> *(526-34)*

If any additional evidence is needed to show that Mosby is not the symbol of evil but is in fact the brilliantly triumphant hero of the poem, Melville's accompanying note should suffice:

> In partisan warfare he proved himself shrewd, able, and enterprising, and always a wary fighter. . . . To our wounded on more than one occasion he showed considerate kindness.

In other words, a major theme of "Bridegroom Dick"— celebration of a manly heart—is also central in "The Scout Toward Aldie." At the campfire, captor and captive acknowledge their equality as heroes:

> "Chickamauga, Feds—take off your hat!"
> "But the Fight in the Clouds repaid you, Rebs!"
> "Forgotten about Manassas yet?"
>
> (507-09)

As in "Bridegroom Dick," Melville dramatizes the large-heartedness he so especially admires by juxtaposing it with its despised opposite, in this case the cold intellectual meanness of a well-named Captain Cloud:

> Ah! why should good fellows foemen be?
> And who would dream that foes they were—
> Larking and singing so friendly then . . .
> But Captain Cloud made sour demur:
> "Guard! keep your prisoners *in* the pen,
> And let none talk with Mosby's men."
>
> . . . down from his brain cold drops distilled,
> Making stalactites in his heart—
> A conscientious soul, forsooth;
> And with a formal hate was filled . . .
>
> (554-66)

A bit earlier, when several Virginians are captured, the

dehumanized nature of the same Captain Cloud is even
more obviously contrasted with the generous spirit of
Captain Morn. They have both just heard a touching
tale of rebel courage and romance:

> "Four walls shall mend that saucy mood,
>   And moping prisons tame him down,"
> Said Captain Cloud. "God help that day,"
> Cried Captain Morn, "and he so young."
>
> *(393-96)*

A similar comment on heartlessness occurs near the out-
set, in an angry portrait of the Hospital Steward whose
calling and uniform protect him from the danger faced
by those around him; he teases "his neighbors of touchy
mood" as they enter the partisan-infested woods:

> He whispered, winked—did all but shout:
> A healthy man for the sick to view . . .
>   Little of care he cared about.
>   And yet of pains and pangs he knew—
> In others . . .
>
> *(86-91)*

Unlike the Steward, the newlywed protagonist goes
eagerly into danger without the protection of "caduceus,
black and green." It is upon Melville's characterization
of the young Colonel, along with that of the hunted
Mosby, that the poem hinges. And, just as Fogle mis-
reads the significance of the partisan leader, so does he
oversimplify that of the Colonel.[16] It is true that the
youth-age differentiation is important here, as through-
out the Civil War poems; the foolhardy young man re-
jects the gray-haired Major's warning, and dies. But it
is not enough to read into this (as Fogle does) a lesson
that survival requires eternal vigilance. The Colonel is
worse than unvigilant: he suffers from the blind, vain-
glorious mania of a Custer—who was nurtured in just

such Civil War excursions and felt unemployed when they came to an end. In fact, Melville's narrative is a chillingly prophetic rehearsal of the Little Big Horn twelve years later, to which he refers in "John Marr" as "a war waged by the Red Men for their native soil and natural rights."

Though a recent bridegroom, the protagonist fails to win our sympathy precisely because Melville has used him to anatomize the growing war-lust in the American spirit, which dismayed him during the rape of Mexico and which he depicted at that time in a prose satire against Zachary Taylor[17] as well as in "the great battle-chant" of *Mardi* called "odious" by Yoomy the bard:

> Sons of battle! Hunters of men!
> Raise high your war-wood!
> Hack away, merry men, hack away.
> Who would not die brave . . . ?
> 'Tis glory that calls
> To each hero that falls . . .

From the moment "the Leader" is introduced, Melville shows fame to be his fatal motive and the military stance his ideal. To a "grizzled Major"—equally brave but wiser after the Seven Days' Fight—

> The Young Man talked (all sworded and spurred)
> Of the partisan's blade he longed to win,
> And frays in which he meant to beat.
>
> (*213-15*)

The Major, sensing that an effort to warn him would be hopeless, leaves the circle of glory-seeking knights doting on their Colonel. Later, however, following the capture of ten "luckless" Mosby-men, the Major can no longer restrain himself, and warns ("Showing a scar by buck-shot made") that the scouting party should clear out while they are ahead. For the partisan-chief is sure

to attempt a rescue: "Look out for Mosby's rifle-crack."
To this, in a tone typical of America's developing war-
mystique, the Colonel replies:

> "We welcome it! give crack for crack!
> Peril, old lad, is what I seek."
>
> *(358-59)*

That other lives beside his own are being gambled is of
no concern to him. Not only the Major voices his sense
of being caught inexorably in a surge of mad militarism;
soon a low whisper rises among the men:

> Young Hair-Brains don't retreat, they say;
> A brush with Mosby is the play!
>
> *(496-97)*

Having galloped deep inside the rebel trap, the Col-
onel responds to the Major's continued warnings by
declaring openly what the Civil War means to him:
"Names must be made and printed be!" Almost imme-
diately afterward, with beautifully narrated suddenness
and craft, the ambushers strike. It is some time before
the death of the Colonel is discovered. He lies—"in a
charm"—cured of his illusions and his hate, along with
the dead at Shiloh and all of Melville's other battle-
fields; and those who survive have suddenly grown wise,
as the hero of "The College Colonel" grew wise in the
Wilderness, the field-hospital, Petersburg crater, and
Libby.

Leon Howard points out the contrast offered in this
poem "between the gaiety of a fresh morning sally and
the moodiness of a weary return,"[18] but this understates
what has really occurred. More fully and graphically
than anywhere else in *Battle-Pieces,* the poet here dra-
matizes the battlefield as a grim classroom—and he does
so even before the guns of Mosby have spoken:

> As restive they turn, how sore they feel,
> And cross, and sleepy, and full of spleen,
> And curse the war. "Fools, North and South!"
> Said one right out.
>
> (*666-69*)

The most obvious contrast is provided by the Colonel himself, the symbol of military adventure:

> *Tan-tara! tan-tara! tan-tara!*
> Mounted and armed he sits a king . . .
>
> (*50-51*)

Thus we see him at first. At the close of his lesson we find him: "Dead! but so calm / That death seemed nothing . . ." His mania is at rest: "Careless of Mosby" he lies, for the first time in the poem. And it is the Major whose one-line elegy takes the measure of such heroism: "The weakest thing is lustihood."

But even more profound is the refining-fire undergone by those who survive. With unmistakable emphasis Melville brings his huge ballad to a close with the dreary burial of the trigger-happy bridegroom, the anguish of his "fame fond" bride, the transformation of the previously self-indulgent and uncompassionate Hospital Steward, and—especially—the shattering of those eager, overconfident "young courtiers" who had admiringly circled "their king" before the sortie:

> The weary troop that wended now—
> Hardly it seemed the same that pricked
> Forth to the forest from the camp . . .
> Each eye dim as a sick-room lamp . . .
> But the wounded cramped in the ambulance,
> It was horror to hear their groans . . .
>
> (*743-68*)

Matthiessen is right[19] to separate Melville's response to

the conflict from that which was "current among the
Northern poets of progress in 1866." Such lines could
have been written "only by a man who had mastered
the meaning of suffering," and—as Matthiessen might
have added—by a man who had long since chosen as his
standard a tuft of kelp.

In "The Scout Toward Aldie," as in "Bridegroom
Dick," Melville introduces other characteristic themes
along with those already noted. One of these, lightly
touched upon rather than preached, is a sense of nature's
uninterested continuity after a human catastrophe (rem-
iniscent of the swallows skimming over the dead in "Shi-
loh" or the gulls, seals, and slug in "The Berg"). Turn-
ing to those crippled in war, Melville felicitously sings:

The froth of the cup is gone for them
(Caw! caw! the crows through the blueness wing) . . .
                                                (67–68)

The same point is made in such shorter Civil War poems
as "The Stone Fleet," "Malvern Hill," "A Requiem for
Soldiers Lost in Ocean Transports," and "On a Natural
Monument in a Field of Georgia." On the other hand,
the poet hints at a more benevolent attitude in the "wild-
ing roses that shed their balm" on the fallen warrior,
and the sweet-fern that "flings an odor nigh" his grave-
yard. This ambivalence underscores his kinship with
Hardy, a younger contemporary, whose "Hap," "The
Subalterns," and "The Convergence of the Twain" ex-
actly parallel Melville's dual view of nature.

Several critics have remarked on Melville's unclear
position with regard to the slavery issue. John Bernstein,
for example, sees reflected in *Mardi* a "divided feeling
towards how to bring about . . . abolition," whether
by warring for freedom or waiting for God.[20] Robert
Penn Warren sees in the war poems a confidence that
resolution will come through nature and history.[21] Cer-

tainly one of the most remarkable facts about the 72 battle-pieces is the scarcity of references to slavery. The agony and heroism produced by the conflict are uppermost in his mind, and at war's end he expresses far greater concern for a reunion between North and South than for the fate of the blacks.[22]

In a score of references to the Rightness of the North and the Wrongness of the South, there is no doubt that the Cause—for Melville no less than for most other Northern poets—is Union rather than Emancipation. Thus, as Andrew Johnson turns out to be a placator of slaveholder sensibilities, Frederick Douglass's bitter disappointment[23] is diametrically opposed by Melville's relief, expressed in a footnote to "The Martyr": ". . . the expectations built hereon . . . happily for the country, have not been verified."[24]

Sidney Kaplan's dissertation[25] centers on this question. He defines Melville as "neither a Sumner nor a Calhoun, neither a Whittier nor a Timrod." But it is necessary to modify the assertion that "from *Typee* to *Battle-Pieces* there is scarcely an important work . . . that does not display Negro men and women or touch in some way on the matter of bondage and revolt." The fact is that in *Battle-Pieces,* where such "display" would seem to be most appropriate, only one supposedly Black man and one Black woman appear. For the rest, there is an indirect poetic allusion in "The Swamp Angel,"[26] a brief note for "A Grave Near Petersburg, Va.,"[27] a not-quite-spelled-out reference to "man's foulest crime,"[28] and a slight, lukewarm questioning of Lee by the Northern Senators (lost amid the lengthy prophecies of "Lee in the Capitol") :

The blacks—should we our arm withdraw,
Would that betray them? some distrust your law.

As for the one man and one woman, they are hard

to place alongside Pip, Fleece, and Babo, whom Charles
H. Nilon[29] in his dissertation ranks "among the most
distinguished character portraits in American literature."
If we are to accept Nilon's conclusion that "Generally,
Melville's Negro characters rise above mere stereotypes,"
the two personages who appear briefly in *Battle-Pieces*
must be dealt with as exceptions. The woman is drawn
at second-hand, from "An Idealized Portrait, By E. Ved-
der." She is the stereotype of the Mammy; although her
face shows "the sufferance of her race. . . . Yet is she not
at strife." For she imagines "the good" which "her
children's children . . . shall know."

A second, far more interesting figure, appears in "The
Scout Toward Aldie." It is Garry, a *Gone With the
Wind* stereotype of the ever-loyal domestic slave, "the
humped driver, black in hue," who is part of a group
captured by the scouting party. In a position to betray
his mistress as the instrument of Mosby's intended trap,
he instead displays a cunning and a personal devotion
which Melville clearly admires. The only freedom Garry
wishes is freedom from the scouting-party. Tersely and
vividly told, this significant episode deserves to be quoted
in full:

> . . . a lame horse, dingy white,
> With clouted harness; ropes in hand,
>   Cringed the humped driver, black in hue . . .
>   (*402-04*)

> The Hospital Steward's turn began:
> "Must squeeze this darkey; every tap
>   Of knowledge we are bound to start."
>   "Garry," she said, "tell all you can
>   Of Colonel Mosby—that brave man."

> "Dun know much, sare; and missis here
>   Know less dan me. But dis I know—"

"Well, what?" "I dun know what I know."
"A knowing answer!" The hump-back coughed,
Rubbing his yellowish wool like tow.
"Come—Mosby—tell!" "O dun look so!
My gal nursed missis—let we go."

"Go where?" demanded Captain Cloud;
"Back into bondage? Man, you're free!"
"Well, *let* we free!" The Captain's brow
Lowered; the Colonel came—had heard:
"Pooh! pooh! his simple heart I see—
A faithful servant . . ."

(*458-75*)

It cannot be overlooked that the one truly anti-slavery
line in the entire Civil War volume should come not from
Melville but from the lips of the poem's most unsympa-
thetic character, Captain Cloud! As for "the humped
driver, black in hue," he turns out to be one of Mosby's
men, his "yellowish wool" a wig!

By far the largest of Melville's ignored poems is the
two-part, 1400-line "Marquis de Grandvin." It too is
based on one of the poet's learning adventures. As "Bride-
groom Dick" memorializes his experience in the U.S.
Navy and "The Scout Toward Aldie" builds on a visit
to the Potomac war front, "Grandvin" springs from the
European tour of 1856-57. A prose overture introduces
a group of New Yorkers who defy post-bellum America
by means of drink and nostalgic talk. Their mentors, the
Marquis de Grandvin and Major Jack Gentian, transport
them: first, with an imagined tavern-debate on aesthetics
among painters of the past; second, with a reminiscence
of pre-Garibaldi Naples.

For those primarily concerned with Melville's craft,

"Grandvin" is interesting on several counts. In the first place, it illustrates his continuing struggle to create a congenial balance, a natural interflow between prose and verse (as in "John Marr," "Rip Van Winkle's Lilac," "Rammon," and *Billy Budd*). Then, too, the representation of differing viewpoints within a narrative tetrameter framework closely resembles the tremendous philosophic debate that is at the core of *Clarel*. Finally, along with much that is musically harsh or overwrought, verbally inappropriate or flat, there occur dozens of individual lines and extended passages that are brilliantly right. If Arvin[30] means to include "Grandvin" among "the larger number of" manuscript poems, he is wrong to dismiss it as "quiet to the point of colorlessness." For Melville lavished as much care on the shaping of these verses as on any of his prose, and they overflow with bursts of imaginative stylistic vigor.

As for their content, it seems to me indispensable—not that it cannot be found elsewhere in Melville, but that its presence in "Grandvin" serves to underscore and clarify. The theme of national reconciliation is a case in point. One scarcely expects to find Civil War references in a work dealing with fine art and an afternoon in old Naples; yet Melville's obsession intrudes in the prose portrayal of his protagonist, Jack Gentian. The Major, though he lost an arm fighting under Grant, shuns the North's annual victory celebration, "even as during the entire military contest, no superfluous syllable ever fell from his lips touching the Southern half of his country." He prefers, somewhat as Melville does in "Aldie," to tell of "the scouting, the foraging, the riding up to lovely mansions garrisoned by a faithful old slave or two, servants to lovely damsels more terrible than Mars in their feminine indignation at the insolent invader." Like Bridegroom Dick, he refuses to condemn the men along with that his reference was not the poem itself but the prose sketches. Yet his is not the only case of negligence. John Bernstein, for example, lists "Grandvin" as though it were a volume;[33] and Howard Vincent, ignoring the internal evidence, declares that "Grandvin" was "undoubtedly" and "especially" what Mrs. Melville meant when she wrote in 1859, "Herman has taken to writing poetry."[34])

Turning to the two-part poem, we find both narrators extolling those qualities which are their own special earmark, while condemning the dominant trend in American life. Grandvin pays tribute to the warmth and honesty of a Jan Steen catholic enough to say: "All's picturesque beneath the sun" yet personally preferring "plain life" to that which is "satin-glossed and flossy-fine." Jolly himself, Steen refuses to judge other sinners "by Pharisee stricture." Franz Hals makes his choice equally clear. Unlike the prudent, calculating Van Dyck, who went to England for patronage, Hals could not be lured from the hearth of home: the open "festival faces" are worth more than the false smiles of kings. "Old friends—old vintages carry the day!" he tells the court portrait-painter "in silken dress / Not smoother than his courteousness . . ."

Similarly Tintoretto ("the dyer's son, / A leoline strength, no strained falsetto") is juxtaposed against Veronese, decked all in gold "Like to a Golden Pheasant." His eye rejects "florid things" in favor of "A thatched hut . . . rotting trees . . . many a grimy slimy lair." At this the "fastidious" and "dainty prim" Carlo Dolce squirms, but Adrian Brouwer, with "ruddled face" and "wine-stained vesture," definitively pronounces the credo of Grandvin-Melville:

. . . haunts that reek may harbor much;
Hey, Teniers? Give us boors at inns,

the cause; sinners are not "demarked from the si
any parallel of latitude."

This magnanimity, demonstrated in "Aldie" a
affirmed by Bridegroom Dick many years later, is
than a political stand. It rises organically from Gen
temperament, his philosophic essence. Charity towar
defeated foe, and a readiness to accept the unpopul
of such a position, go hand in hand with the cluste
qualities listed lovingly by Melville and hatefully by '
ambidextrous double-dealers," the "merchant and ves\
man," whom he satirizes in his prose sketches. O1
again the poet contrasts a cunning self-interest that
leading his nation down the road to Hell, and a sublin
disinterestedness, quite out of fashion, which is America\
one hope for salvation. Both Grandvin and Gentian ar\
noted for their "fine, open, cheery aspect," their love o1
good wine and "good fellowship," their "genial humor,"
their reverence for forgotten glories, their "cosmopolitan\
sympathies," their true Christianity devoid of cant and
posturing, their ability to inspire "gentle charities, brave
conceptions, heroic virtues." They resemble Bridegroom
Dick's particular hero, Genteel Jack, "All bland *poli-
tesse*," their lives—like his watch-chain—"with love's
jeweled tokens abounding."

When a Grandvin invents a wassail involving greatly
differing ghost-artists, we can be sure it will be more than
what Melville himself drolly calls "an inconclusive debate
as to the exact import" of the term *picturesque*.[31] Then,
when a Jack Gentian takes the floor ("how frolic, pa-
thetic, indignant, philosophic; and throughout how catho-
lic and humane"), we should expect more than a retro-
spective review of "certain convivial days and nights in
the old times"[32]—as Warner Berthoff inaccurately char-
acterizes it. (By titling it "An Afternoon in Naples"
rather than "Naples in the Time of Bomba," he indicates

Mud floor—dark settles—jugs—old bins,
Under rafters foul with fume that blinks
From logs too soggy much to blaze
Which yet diffuse an umberish haze
That beautifies the grime, methinks.

(*281-87*)

The poet is not advocating boorishness or escape from
reality, but he sees the tavern hour as necessary for sur-
vival in a difficult world, and wine as a mellowing force
which opens the heart to the duality of existence. This
theme is also developed in "Naples in the Time of
Bomba." Perhaps, Melville suggests, the duality of dove
and adder seethes within the wine itself, for the vines of
Naples "take hot flavor / From Vesuvius," and their
grape

Drowneth thinking,
Every night-fall,
Heard in Strada,
Kiss the doves
And coos the adder!

(*358-62*)

Naples as a geographical lure is itself such a wine:

. . . such Nature all about!
No surly moor of forge and mill,
She charms us glum barbarians still,
Fleeing from frost, bad bread, or duns,
Despotic *Biz*, and devils blue . . .

(*167-71*)

Yet Naples does not provide Gentian-Melville with
the sense of peace he craves. The tourist's illusion of
joy keeps being wrecked by the ugly sorties of King Bom-
ba's troops and by his own "scarce cheerful" review of
human history. Thus, when a flower-girl sells him a rose,

a counterpoint is set off within his mind that lasts throughout the poem (very much like the Callicles-Empedocles interplay of intuition and feeling versus overintellectuality in Matthew Arnold's *Empedocles on Etna*):

Come, take thine ease; lean back, my soul;
The world let spin; what signifies?
Look, she, the flower-girl—what recks she
Of Bomba's sortie? what indeed!

(*239-42*)

It is important that Melville annotated closely his copy of Arnold's grim poem; that, at the outset of his European travels, Melville told Hawthorne "he had pretty much made up his mind to be annihilated";[35] that the appeals of the Rose are no more effective with the depressed tourist in Naples than are the appeals of Callicles as Empedocles ascends Etna. But it is more important that Melville did not jump into the crater, that he chose to be a poet, that he kept working at the materials of his travels until he was able to modulate his "powerful and sometimes despairing reaction to the cruel irreconcilables of life," as Richard Chase puts it.[36]

Ultimately he achieved the elusive balance that could be embodied in the remarkable Major Jack Gentian, a protagonist capable of illuminating—with the help of wit and wine—Melville's dark afternoon in Naples. We see, then, that the quaffing of burgundy or the smoking of Herba Santa is not, for Melville, an approach to stupefaction, but an act of cameraderie and a defense against the kinds of over-thinking that are sterile or destructive: *Biz* on the one hand, Empedoclean despair on the other.

To those who use their wakeful hours prudently, it is shocking that a man of talent should "waste himself" at the cups. He becomes so foolishly mellow, they gasp, that he converses with vagabonds and ends up "bestowing something" upon them. To this Melville replies: "Thou mayest *outlive thy usefulness* (execrable phrase!) but never thy loving-kindness." We have already seen the extent of the poet's compassion as he describes the wounded in "The Scout Toward Aldie." In "At the Hostelry" Tintoretto expresses concern for those in "Rome's squalid ghetto" and at the lazaretto of Algiers. Two graphic examples of the poet's sensitivity to suffering occur in "Bomba." Under the surface gaiety of the ragamuffs he sees "a patched despair, / Bravery in tatters debonair, / True devil-may-care dilapidation." Later he focuses on a Levant boy who warns the people that the soldiers are coming. Such boys are far from angels: some are "Arch imps of Pandarus," others pick pockets "with small brown fingers slim / Busier than the jackdaw's bill." But, like Jan Steen, Gentian-Melville does not judge sinners; he loves them, commiserates with them, speaks for them:

A weed of life, a sea-weed he . . .
Who, in repletion's lust for more,
And penury's strife for daily bread,
As licensed by compassionate heaven
To privateer it on their wits,
The Mid Sea rove from quay to quay . . .

(485-92)

This wry comment on a "compassionate heaven" underscores the contrasts between Gentian's professed freethinking on the one hand and truly Christian behavior on the other; between the professed Christianity of "the respectable vestryman" and his un-Christian, money-minded hardness. Leon Howard is surprised to find in the poem "some traces of his earlier antagonism toward formalized religion . . . curiously out of place among his later works . . ."[37] That this antagonism is not out of place but very much a part of his later works, is proven in "The New Ancient of Days," "Montaigne and His

Kitten," "Stockings in the Farm-House Chimney," "The New Rosicrucians," "The New Zealot to the Sun," "The Margrave's Birthnight," and other poems, but especially in "Rip Van Winkle's Lilac," which Howard[38] dates in the late '80s and relates to Jack Gentian (it actually belongs with "At the Hostelry").

The crux of "Rip Van Winkle" is an encounter between an artist painting "a miserable old ruin" under a "half-rotten lilac-tree" (à la Tintoretto), and a "hatchet-faced stony-eyed" Pharisee who first suggests that "something godly . . . our new tabernacle" be painted instead, and finally thunders: "Providence will take you in hand one of these days . . . " This allegorical figure is recognized by the artist as Death "in the guise of a living man."

In "Grandvin" the attacks on organized religion take three forms. First, in the prologue to "At the Hostelry," Melville celebrates Italy's liberation from the divisive, paralyzing force of "cowls misguided":

Ancona, plucked from Peter's Chair,
With all the Papal fiefs in band . . .
In Rome no furtive cloaked one now
Scribbles his gibe on Pasquin's brow,
Since wag his tongue at Popes who may
The Popedom needs endure his say.

(73-83)

Second, in "Bomba," through the Levant boy's intelligent glance which takes in "The motley miscellaneous groups" on a Naples thoroughfare, Melville creates a collective portrait as vividly sardonic as Chaucer:

Fat monk with paunched umbrella blue;
The quack, magnific in brocade . . .
A Jesuit grave, genteely sleek
In dapper small-clothes and fine hose
Of sable silk, and shovel-hat;

Hard by a doctor of the law,
In sables, too, with parchment cheek;
A useful man to lawless power,
Expert to legalise the wrong.
The twain, brief tarrying there behind,
Went sauntering off . . .

(518-46)

The third approach is more depressed than satiric. Both
in tone and imagery it is related to "The Margrave's
Birthnight." Following a military sortie, the tourist's
hopes are momentarily lifted by the people's "Grinding
their teeth at Bomba's guards"; but anon comes a re-
ligious procession:

It comes; a corpulent form erect . . .
And, under this [canopy], a shining priest
Who to some death-bed bears the *host*
In mystic state before him veiled.

A hush falls; and the people drop . . .

(695-706)

Gentian-Melville's hopes drop too, for the throng, "trans-
fixed" by ritual, bow over like "Pompeiian masquers"
caught in the act of flight, "For ages glued in deadly
drift." With this, the Rose that had been trying to lift
his spirit, expires: "its soul / Of musk dissolved in
empty air!"

Clearly, Gentian-Melville loves what is past not for
the sake of its age—mark his rejection of old ritual when
it is hollow, when it paralyzes rather than inspires, when
it is used as a political instrument. Like his brother
Quixote in "The Rusty Man," Gentian idolizes what has
been discarded as "useless" by a crass Present irked at
being reminded of a nobler Past. As the "wronged one's
knight" unprosperously gropes " 'Mong his old folios" in

search of chivalry's "obsolete saws," so are Jack Gen-
tian's "musty old romances" derided by the thriving
"grocer green" of Melville's day, "a young Croesus of
complexion pink and white."

True to his autumnal name, Gentian loves "the historic
Past," and Grandvin, true to his, "never is so . . . bliss-
fully serene, as when wandering in a haze along that en-
chanted beach." In exactly the elegiac tone of Bridegroom
Dick, and also addressing an audience of one, Major Jack
pays touching tribute both to the forgotten hero of Mon-
terey, "a homespun paladin, General Worth," and its
forgotten poet, his "chivalric friend" Charles Fenno
Hoffman.[39] Rebuke is implied in the comment that the
General's "*worth* was of another sort than that of the
purse," and that we "don't go back so far" as to recall
a fine poet of thirty years ago.

The rebuke sharpens in the poem itself. As William
Plomer points out, "Nostalgia could bring out his pow-
ers as a poet."[40] This it does because it is a militant nos-
talgia, at war against "the way of the world in his day"
and the direction in which it is headed. Garibaldi's knight-
liness shines "like phosphorus scratched in dark" against
the "grimed walls" of an age "Where scarce in vogue are
'Plutarch's Men,' / And jobbers deal in popular glory."
As Ungar does in *Clarel*, Grandvin (in a sequel to "At
the Hostelry") questions the possibility of heroism in
the "treadmill-Paradise" that is coming, the "Millenium
of the busy bee" toward which "the levellers scything
move . . ." When there are no Tarquins to challenge,
"What plumed career" could a Garibaldi-Cid-St. George
have?

Never he'd quit his trading trips,
Perchance, would fag in trade at desk,
Or, slopped in slimy slippery sludge,

Lifelong on Staten Island drudge,
Melting his tallow . . .

(*631-35*)

Deploring the spiritual bankruptcy toward which his world is moving, Melville concludes with a prayer that the future not only bring material benefits, but also "sprinkle . . . some drops of grace / Nor polish us into commonplace."

At times the protest is muted; remarkably close to the spirit and language of Bridegroom Dick's elegy for the hearts-of-oak era, is Van der Velde's dirge for "the departed three-deckers of De Ruyter and Van Trump." Here, as throughout "At the Hostelry," Melville manages simultaneously to explore the essence of a painter and to turn the exploration into a resonant poetic symbol through which his own credo is enunciated. Van der Velde, like some cast-off lion-heart of old, like the poet himself, muses "on glories engulfed in the Past." He has seen "morn's rays slant 'twixt the bones / Of the oaken *Dunderberg* broken up." To this the "grocer green" mentality of a Gerald Douw responds that he too appreciates old oak—not on three-deckers, but "in kitchen-dresser . . . set out with . . . well scoured sauce-pans."

Seldom in Melville's writings is the triumphant doctrine of utilitarianism more tellingly opposed than in "At the Hostelry." The very idea of bothering to define the Picturesque has become obsolete, meaningless:

In peacocks' tails put out the eyes!
Utility reigns—Ah, well-a-way!—
And bustles along in Bentham's shoes.
For the Picturesque—suffice, suffice
The picture that fetches a picturesque price!

(*122-26*)

This is Grandvin-Melville raging directly to his super-
annuated Burgundians. Later, at mention of Venice's
glory, Veronese declares to a sympathetic Watteau:

This cabbage *Utility, parbleu!*
What shall insure the Carnival—
The gondola—the Grand Canal?
That palaced duct they'll yet deplete,
Improve it to a huckster's street . . .
(475-79)

The hostelry conjured up by Grandvin's imagination
is "the Inn of Inns," not unlike that "Mermaid in the
Zodiac" celebrated by Keats with the same romantic
yearning, and Bridegroom Dick's parlor "In Paradise
. . . where the even tempers be." Here on earth a tav-
ern offers frail defense against the rawness outside. But
at the eternal cups,

Never comes the mart's intrusive roar,
Nor heard the shriek that starts the train,
Nor teasing telegraph clicks again,
No news is cried, and hurry is no more . . .
(559-62)

This sounds like the Shelleyan ache for escape into death.
The inn-symbol corresponds to "Bomba," where, signifi-
cantly quoting the proverb, "See Naples, and—then die,"
Melville describes the Neapolitan islands as a foretaste
of "The floating Isles of Paradise." On the surface this
would seem to support Parrington's view of Melville[41]
as an "arch romantic" who "vainly sought to erect his
romantic dreams as a defense against reality." But a
look at "Grandvin" shows the opposite to be true.

Both "At the Hostelry" and "Bomba" refute Parring-
ton's assertion that the poet "was not concerned about
politics or the political state." (Perhaps he meant to say
that Melville's democratism, like Jack Gentian's, was

"less of the stump than the heart.") "At the Hostelry"
opens with a hundred-line tribute to Garibaldi and Ca-
vour—apparently unrelated to the poem itself—which
shows that Melville followed Risorgimento politics
closely and enthusiastically.

As for "Naples in the Time of Bomba," it is richly
interlarded with political comment. Warmly received in
"Bomba's Naples," the tourist wonders whether "Those
shocking stories" about "dire tyranny in Naples" were
perhaps exaggerated. Yet the castle's "surly walls" seem
designed "Less to beat alien foemen off / Than awe the
town," and from them suddenly stream a thousand
troops:

Sicilians from Palermo shipped
In meet exchange for hirelings lent
From Naples here to hold the Isle . . .
To threaten, intimidate, and cow.

(116–21)

Noting the people's hatred in their "mutterings like deep
thunder low," Gentian-Melville forecasts a storm.

Despite the city's sensual distractions, he cannot help
remembering an earlier storm roused by oppression. In
an arresting passage on the cyclical agony of history, he
calls the 1647 rebellion—when a Naples mob beheaded
its young leader—a "portent" of 1793 and of later
events inspired by France:

Red after-years, and whirl of error
When Freedom linkt with Furies raved
In Carmagnole and cannibal hymn,
Mad song and dance before the ark
From France imported with *The Terror!* . . .
Hell's cornucopia crammed with crime!

(463–69)

Any discussion of "The House-Top," Melville's re-

sponse to the 1863 anti-draft riots, should take these
lines into account.[42] But the "Wise Draco" summoned to
end New York's massacre is a far cry from Bomba's
marvelously spoofed drum-major:

In aigulets and tinsel tags—
Pagoda glittering in Cathay!
Arch whiskerando and gigantic . . .
Tossing his truncheon in the van . . .
Barbaric in his bearskin shako . . .
A braggadocio Bourbon-Draco!

(624–33)

It is typical that, in his intense awareness of duality, Mel-
ville should place the terrible and the ludicrous side by
side, that he should celebrate "gyved Naples" on a day
when "She sobbed, she laughed, she rattled her chain."
For such, he tells us, is the politics of Place. As for the
politics of Time, what better example than Garibaldi—
who soon enough brought the predicted storm down upon
tyranny's head, and was himself soon enough a ghost?
"Pale glory walks by valor's bier." I am suggesting that
politics, like every other aspect of the human condition,
interested Melville deeply; but—with his transcendental
reverence for the essential, the general—he tried to see
it as symptom and symbol.

The overriding value of "Naples in the Time of Bom-
ba" is that it reveals, more dramatically and fully than
the travel journals, Melville's state of mind in early
1857.[43] For it is about this time that his thinking veers
from "annihilation" to recommitment. What he seizes
upon in Egypt, in Greece, in Italy—be it pyramid,
acropolis, or the ghost of Tasso—becomes the cumula-
tive sustaining model for his new career as poet, a career
of "quiet heroism," in Chase's words.[44]

Already in "Bomba" he dives, "mid loud gregarious
lies," for the bitter weed of Truth, accepting loneness

and pain, wrestling "with the angel—Art" for a fusion
of "unlike things."[45] He peers into Vesuvius's crater,
tastes its ash; but instead of jumping in, like Empedo-
cles, or dying of the bitterness, like Mortmain in *Clarel,*
or impotently railing against "The ever-upbubbling wick-
edness," like Ungar, he endures and announces his find-
ings within that "sulphurious Hill / Whose vent far
hellward reaches down!" Lush, alluring, carefree Naples
itself becomes a symbol:

Type ye what Naples is alway?
Yes, round these curved volcanic shores,
Vined urn of ashes, bed on bed,
Abandonment as thoughtless pours
As when the revelling pagan led.

(*285-89*)

For the vines "take hot flavor / From Vesuvius"; the
sulphur and "the black grape" rise from one pit.

It is suggested that Pisa's leaning tower reminded
Melville, in March 1857, of his old self: "shivering on
the verge, / A would-be suicide!" If that is so, then the
sight of the Parthenon in February stirred a counter-
current, for he saw the temple as a testing and shaping
force that might have countered a Diogenes's cynicism.
This affirmative current gathered force as he followed
Tasso's career from the home in Sorrento to the prison
in Ferrara to the deathbed in Rome.[46] Where the Pales-
tine pilgrimage fails, the search for Tasso's ghost suc-
ceeds, for out of it comes the definition of a poet's tor-
ment and triumph, and it is this definition, restated in a
score of his noblest poems, which keeps Melville lyri-
cally alive for the next 35 years.

During the critical time recorded in "Bomba," the
poet visited Virgil's supposed burial-place at Pausilippo,
near Naples, and wrote in his journal: "at Posilipo [sic]
found not the cessation which the name expresses" [eas-

ing pain—Greek].[47] Virgil, however, he bitterly implies
in "Bomba," assuredly found ease—not only because he
is dead but because he was—unlike a Tasso or a Camo-
ëns or a Melville—"Rome's laureate in Rome's palmy
time," who produced what Rome wished to hear: "vol-
umed numbers rolling bland."

Here Melville typically pits the ancient laureate
against a modern prophet, a foe of tyranny whose body
and spirit were recently crushed in a series of prisons.
Although the actual Silvio Pellico is three years dead,
Gentian-Melville invents a glimpse of "the quelled en-
thusiast . . . / Unmanned, made meek through strenu-
ous wrong." Pellico also appears in a *Timoleon* poem
called "Pausilippo (In the Time of Bomba)." The piece,
however, is clearly an extract from "Naples in the Time
of Bomba." I believe Melville included it in the 1891
collection because it illustrates, along with so many other
poems in *Timoleon,* what can happen to a poet whose
mind is (as he says of another poet in an 1885 letter)
"utterly untrameled [sic] and independent":[48]

Clandestine arrest abrupt by night;
The sole conjecturable cause
The yearning in a patriot ode
Construed as treason; trial none;
Prolonged captivity profound . . .

The same Melville who peered into Vesuvius, who
chose between the laureateship of Virgil and the martyr-
dom of Pellico, delved for personal meaning in the
museum-paintings of Europe. Thus, "At the Hostelry"
expresses far less Melville's "lifelong interest in paint-
ing,"[49] as Leon Howard believes, than the continuing
effort to define his life.

As such, it deserves the most careful scrutiny. The
reader must "clue in" on the way Melville describes each
artist and on the way each formulates his argument. The
rewards of such a reading are great indeed. One dis-

covers that, as in *Clarel*, although Melville seems to be
presenting a variety of views and life-styles without com-
mitting himself to any, the debate is not nearly so "in-
conclusive" as our tongue-in-cheek poet says. It is the
"strong" Tintoretto ("Titan work by him was done")
who touches the central nerve of Melville's belief:
"Some decay must lurk: / In florid things but small its
share." It is the "thriftless" Jan Steen, "fellowly yet
thoughtful," who expresses the poet's catholicity:

> . . . all's picture; death and life
> Pictures and pendants, nor at strife—
> No, never to hearts that muse thereon . . .
> . . . the life that's *wine and brine,*
> The mingled brew; the thing as spanned
> By Jan who kept the Leyden tavern
> And every rollicker fellowly scanned—
> And, under his vineyard, lo, a cavern!
>   (*434–44*)

This Vesuvian image—the courage to breathe sulphur
—is marvelously demonstrated by Spagnoletto, who
"raised his head / From sombre musings, and revealed /
A brow by no blest angel sealed." At mention of the
poisoner Borgia, he instantly imagines a great painting
(or poem) on the nature of wickedness:

> . . . let His Grace
> Be launching, ay, the loving-cup
> Among the princes in the hall
> At Sinigaglia: You recall?
> I mean those gudgeons whom his smile
> Flattered to sup, ere yet awhile,
> In Hades with Domitian's lords.
>
> Let sunny frankness charm his air,
> His raiment lace with silver cords,
> Trick forth the *'Christian statesman'* there.

And, mind ye, don't forget the pall;
Suggest it—how politeness ended:
Let lurk in shade of rearward wall
Three bravoes by the arras splendid.

(392–405)

This is the artist's role Melville affirms,[50] just as he
rejects Van Dyck, "In whose well-polished gentle mien /
The practiced courtier of Kings was seen," and Veronese,
"In feather high, in fortune free," awarded "a jeweled
hilt" for his flowery gilt canvases, and especially Rubens,
well-rewarded for his "Peachy and plump" Venus—"a
canvas meet for donor":

The Knight, Sir Peter Paul, 'twas he,
Hatted in rich felt, spick and span,
Right comely in equipment free
With court-air of Lord Chamberlain . . .

(352–55)

Here, then, in its most extended and graphic expres-
sion, is the central contrast—enunciated elsewhere in
lyric after lyric: the contrast between those "discreet"
ones who "trudge where worldlings go" and those "lone"
ones who will not "shrink from Truth . . . Mid loud
gregarious lies" ("The Enthusiast"); between those who
"keep their strength in prudent place" and those who
fall exhausted as they "Hunt . . . the flying herd of
themes" ("Camoëns"); between those who "turn with
weather of the time" and those who "Stand where Pos-
terity shall stand" ("Lone Founts"); between those
who heap "Gems and jewels" and those who "grapple
from Art's deep / One dripping trophy!" ("In a Gar-
ret"); between the Rose Farmer who boasts a sure
market for his "heaps of posies" and his unpopular,
impractical neighbor, "lean as a rake," who

with painstaking throes
Essays to crystallize the rose.

Bridegroom Dick

1876

Sunning ourselves in October on a day
Balmy as spring, though the year was in decay,
I lading my pipe, she stirring her tea,
My old woman she says to me,
"Feel ye, old man, how the season mellows?"
And why should I not, blessed heart alive,
Here mellowing myself, past sixty-five,
To think o' the May-time o' pennoned young fellows
This stripped old hulk here for years may survive.

Ere yet, long ago, we were spliced, Bonny Blue,   *10*
(Silvery it gleams down the moon-glade o' time,
Ah, sugar in the bowl and berries in the prime!)
Coxswain I o' the Commodore's crew,—
Under me the fellows that manned his fine gig,
Spinning him ashore, a king in full fig.
Chirrupy even when crosses rubbed me,
Bridegroom Dick lieutenants dubbed me.
Pleasant at a yarn, Bob O'Linkum in a song,
Diligent in duty and nattily arrayed,
Favored I was, wife, and *fleeted* right along;   *20*
And though but a tot for such a tall grade,
A high quartermaster at last I was made.

All this, old lassie, you have heard before,

49

But you listen again for the sake e'en o' me;
No babble stales o' the good times o' yore
To Joan, if Darby the babbler be.

Babbler?—O' what? Addled brains, they forget!
O—quartermaster I; yes, the signals set,
Hoisted the ensign, mended it when frayed,
Polished up the binnacle, minded the helm,   *30*
And prompt every order blithely obeyed.
To me would the officers say a word cheery—
Break through the starch o' the quarter-deck realm;
His coxswain late, so the Commodore's pet.
Ay, and in night-watches long and weary,
Bored nigh to death with the naval etiquette,
Yearning, too, for fun, some younker, a cadet,
Dropping for time each vain bumptious trick,
Boylike would unbend to Bridegroom Dick.
But a limit there was—a check, d'ye see: *40*
Those fine young aristocrats knew their degree.

Well, stationed aft where their lordships keep,—
Seldom going forward excepting to sleep,—
I, boozing now on by-gone years,
My betters recall along with my peers.
Recall them? Wife, but I see them plain:
Alive, alert, every man stirs again.
Ay, and again on the lee-side pacing,
My spy-glass carrying, a truncheon in show,
Turning at the taffrail, my footsteps retracing,   *50*
Proud in my duty, again methinks I go.
And Dave, Dainty Dave, I mark where he stands,
Our trim sailing-master, to time the high-noon,
That thingumbob sextant perplexing eyes and hands,
Squinting at the sun, or twigging o' the moon;
Then, touching his cap to Old Chock-a-Block
Commanding the quarter-deck,—"Sir, twelve o'clock."

Where sails he now, that trim sailing-master,
Slender, yes, as the ship's sky-s'l pole?
Dimly I mind me of some sad disaster—   *60*
Dainty Dave was dropped from the navy-roll!
And ah, for old Lieutenant Chock-a-Block—
Fast, wife, chock-fast to death's black dock!
Buffeted about the obstreperous ocean,
Fleeted his life, if lagged his promotion.
Little girl, they are all, all gone, I think,
Leaving Bridegroom Dick here with lids that wink.

Where is Ap Catesby? The fights fought of yore
Famed him, and laced him with epaulets, and more.
But fame is a wake that after-wakes cross,   *70*
And the waters wallow all, and laugh *Where's the loss?*
But John Bull's bullet in his shoulder bearing
Ballasted Ap in his long seafaring.
The middies they ducked to the man who had messed
With Decatur in the gun-room, or forward pressed
Fighting beside Perry, Hull, Porter, and the rest.

Humped veteran o' the Heart-o'-Oak war,
Moored long in haven where the old heroes are,
Never on *you* did the iron-clads jar!
Your open deck when the boarder assailed,   *80*
The frank old heroic hand-to-hand then availed.

But where's Guert Gan? Still heads he the van?
As before Vera-Cruz, when he dashed splashing through
The blue rollers sunned, in his brave gold-and-blue,
And, ere his cutter in keel took the strand,
Aloft waved his sword on the hostile land!
Went up the cheering, the quick chanticleering;
All hands vying—all colors flying:
"Cock-a-doodle-doo!" and "Row, boys, row!"
"Hey, Starry Banner!" "Hi, Santa Anna!"—   *90*

Old Scott's young dash at Mexico.
Fine forces o' the land, fine forces o' the sea,
Fleet, army, and flotilla—tell, heart o' me,
Tell, if you can, whereaway now they be!

But ah, how to speak of the hurricane unchained—
The Union's strands parted in the hawser over-strained;
Our[51] flag blown to shreds, anchors gone altogether—
The dashed fleet o' States in Secession's foul weather.

Lost in the smother o' that wide public stress,
In hearts, private hearts, what ties there were
    snapped!   *100*
Tell, Hal——vouch, Will, o' the ward-room mess,
On you how the riving thunder-bolt clapped.
With a bead in your eye and beads in your glass,
And a grip o' the flipper, it was part and pass:
"Hal, must it be; Well, if come indeed the shock,
To North or to South, let the victory cleave,
Vaunt it he may on his dung-hill the cock,
But *Uncle Sam's* eagle never crow will, believe."

Sentiment: ay, while suspended hung all,
Ere the guns against Sumter opened there the ball,   *110*
And partners were taken, and the red dance began,
War's red dance o' death!—Well, we, to a man,
We sailors o' the North, wife, how could we lag?—
Strike with your kin, and you stick to the flag!
But to sailors o' the South that easy way was barred.
To some, dame, believe (and I speak o' what I know),
Wormwood the trial and the Uzzite's black shard;
And the faithfuller the heart, the crueller the throe.
Duty? It pulled with more than one string,
This way and that, and anyhow a sting.   *120*
The flag and your kin, how be true unto both?
If either plight ye keep, then ye break the other troth.

But elect here they must, though the casuists were out;
Decide—hurry up—and throttle every doubt.

Of all these thrills thrilled at keelson, and throes,
Little felt the shoddyites a-toasting o' their toes;
In mart and bazaar Lucre chuckled the huzza,
Coining the dollars in the bloody mint of war.
But in men, gray knights o' the Order o' Scars,
And brave boys bound by vows unto Mars,   *130*
Nature grappled honor, intertwisting in the strife:—
But some cut the knot with a thoroughgoing knife.
For how when the drums beat? How in the fray
In Hampton Roads on the fine balmy day?

There a lull, wife, befell—drop o' silence in the din.
Let us enter that silence ere the belchings re-begin.—
Through a ragged rift aslant in the cannonade's smoke
An iron-clad reveals her repellent broadside
Bodily intact. But a frigate, all oak,
Shows honeycombed by shot, and her deck crimson-
    dyed.   *140*

And a trumpet from port of the iron-clad hails,
Summoning the other, whose flag never trails:
"Surrender that frigate, Will! Surrender,
Or I will sink her—*ram,* and end her!"

'T was Hal. And Will, from the naked heart-o'-oak,
Will, the old messmate, minus trumpet, spoke,
Informally intrepid,—"Sink her, and be damned!"*

Enough. Gathering way, the iron-clad *rammed.*
The frigate, heeling over, on the wave threw a dusk.
Not sharing in the slant, the clapper of her bell   *150*
The fixed metal struck[52]—uninvoked struck the knell

---

* Historic [Melville's note]

Of the *Cumberland* stilettoed by the *Merrimac's* tusk;
While, broken in the wound underneath the gun-deck,
Like a sword-fish's blade in leviathan waylaid,
The tusk was left infixed in the fast-foundering wreck.
There, dungeoned[53] in the cockpit, the wounded go down,
And the chaplain with them.[54] But the surges[55] uplift
The prone dead from[56] deck, and for moment they drift
Washed with the swimmers, and the spent swimmers
    drown.
Nine fathom did she sink,—erect, though hid from
    light   *160*
Save her colors unsurrendered[57] and spars that kept
    the height.

Nay, pardon,[58] old aunty! Wife,[59] never let it fall,
That big started tear that hovers on the brim;
I forgot about your nephew and the *Merrimac's* ball;
No more then of her, since it summons up him.

But talk o' fellows' hearts in the wine's genial cup:—
Trap them in the fate, jam them in the strait,
Guns speak their hearts then, and speak right up.

The troublous colic o' intestine war
It sets the bowels o' affection ajar.   *170*
But, lord, old dame, so spins the whizzing world,
A humming-top, ay, for the little boy-gods
Flogging it well with their smart little rods,
Tittering at time and the coil uncurled.

Now, now, sweetheart, you sidle away,
No, never you like *that* kind o' *gay;*
But sour if I get, giving truth her due,
Honey-sweet forever, wife, will Dick be to *you!*

But avast with the War! Why recall racking days

Since set[60] up anew are the ship's started stays?   *180*
Nor less, though the gale we have left behind,
Well may the heave o' the sea remind.
It irks me now, as it troubled me then,
To think o' the fate in the madness o' men.
If Dick was with Farragut on the night-river,
When the boom-chain we burst in the fire-raft's glare,
That blood-dyed the visage as red as the liver;
In the *Battle for the Bay* too if Dick had a share,
And saw one aloft a-piloting the war—
Trumpet in the whirlwind, a Providence in place—   *190*
Our Admiral old whom the captains huzza,
Dick joys in the man nor brags about the race.

But better, wife, I like to bowse on the days
Ere the Old Order foundered in these very frays,
And tradition was lost and we learned strange ways.
Often I think on the brave cruises then;
Re-sailing them in memory, I hail the press o' men
On the gunned promenade where rolling they go,
Ere the dog-watch expire and break up the show.
The Laced Caps I see between forward guns;   *200*
Away from the powder-room they puff the cigar;
"Three days more, hey, the donnas and the dons!"
"Your Xeres widow, will you hunt her up, Starr?"
The Laced Caps laugh, and the bright waves too;
Very jolly, very wicked, both sea and crew,
Nor heaven looks sour on either, I guess,
Nor Pecksniff he bosses the gods' high mess.

Wistful ye peer, wife, concerned for my head,
And how best to get me betimes to my bed.

But king o' the club, the gayest golden spark,   *210*
Sailor o' sailors, what sailor do I mark?
Tom Tight, Tom Tight, no fine fellow finer,

A cutwater-nose, ay, a spirited soul;
But, bowsing away at the well-brewed bowl,
He never bowled back from that last voyage to China.
Tom was lieutenant in the brig-o'-war famed
When an officer was hung for an arch-mutineer,
But a mystery cleaved, and the captain was blamed,
And a rumpus too raised, though his honor it was clear.
And Tom he would say, when the mousers would
    try him,   *220*
And with cup after cup o' Burgundy ply him:
"Gentlemen, in vain with your wassail you beset,
For the more I tipple, the tighter do I get."
No blabber, no, not even with the can—
True to himself and loyal to his clan.

Tom blessed us starboard and d—d us larboard,
Right down from rail to the streak o' the garboard.
Nor less, wife, we liked him.—Tom was a man
In contrast queer with Chaplain Le Fan,
Who blessed us at morn, and at night yet again,   *230*
D—ning us only in decorous strain;
Preaching 'tween the guns—each cutlass in its place—
From text that averred old Adam a hard case.
I see him—Tom—on *horse-block* standing,
Trumpet at mouth, thrown up all amain,
An elephant's bugle, vociferous demanding
Of topmen aloft in the hurricane of rain,
"Letting that sail there your faces flog?
Manhandle it, men, and you'll get the good grog!"
O Tom, but he knew a blue-jacket's ways,   *240*
And how a lieutenant may genially haze;
Only a sailor sailors heartily praise.

Wife, where be all these chaps, I wonder?
Trumpets in the tempest, terrors in the fray,

Boomed their commands along the deck like thunder;
But silent is the sod, and thunder dies away.

But Captain Turret, *"Old Hemlock"* tall,
(A leaning tower when his tank brimmed all,)
Manoeuvre out alive from the war did he?
Or, too old for that, drift under the lee?   *250*
Kentuckian colossal, who, touching at Madeira,
The huge puncheon shipped o' prime *Santa-Clara;*
Then rocked along the deck so solemnly!
No whit the less though judicious was enough
In dealing with the Finn who made the great huff;
Our three-decker's giant, a grand boatswain's mate,
Manliest of men in his own natural senses;
But driven stark mad by the devil's drugged stuff,
Storming all aboard from his run-ashore late,
Challenging to battle, vouchsafing no pretenses,   *260*
A reeling King Ogg, delirious in power,
The quarter-deck carronades he seemed to make cower.
"Put him in *brig* there!" said Lieutenant Marrot.
"Put him in *brig!*" back he mocked like a parrot;
"Try it, then!" swaying a fist like Thor's sledge,
And making the pigmy constables hedge—
Ship's corporals and the master-at-arms.
"In *brig* there, I say!"—They dally no more;
Like hounds let slip on a desperate boar,
Together they pounce on the formidable Finn,   *270*
Pinion and cripple and hustle him in.
Anon, under sentry, between twin guns,
He slides off in drowse, and the long night runs.

Morning brings a summons. Whistling it calls,
Shrilled through the pipes of the boatswain's four aids;
Thrilled down the hatchways along the dusk halls:
Muster to the Scourge!—Dawn of doom and its blast!

As from cemeteries raised, sailors swarm before the mast,
Tumbling up the ladders from the ship's nether shades.

Keeping in the background and taking small part,   *280*
Lounging at their ease, indifferent in face,
Behold the trim marines uncompromised in heart;
Their Major, buttoned up, near the staff finds room—
The staff o' lieutenants standing grouped in their place.
All the Laced Caps o' the ward-room come,
The Chaplain among them, disciplined and dumb.
The blue-nosed boatswain, complexioned like slag,
Like a blue Monday lours[61]—his implements in bag.
Executioners, his aids, a couple by him stand,
At a nod there the thongs to receive from his hand.   *290*
Never venturing a caveat whatever may betide,
Though functionally here on humanity's side,
The grave Surgeon shows, like the formal physician
Attending the rack o'the Spanish Inquisition.

The angel o' the "brig" brings his prisoner up;
Then, steadied by his old *Santa-Clara,* a sup,
Heading all erect, the ranged assizes there,
Lo, Captain Turret, and under starred bunting,
(A florid full face and fine silvered hair,)
Gigantic the yet greater giant confronting.   *300*

Now the culprit he liked, as a tall captain can
A Titan subordinate and true *sailor-man;*
And frequent he'd shown it—no worded advance,
But flattering the Finn with a well-timed glance.
But what of that now? In the martinet-mien
Read the *Articles of War,* heed the naval routine;
While, cut to the heart a dishonor there to win,
Restored to his senses, stood the Anak Finn;
In racked self-control the squeezed tears peeping,

Scalding the eye with repressed inkeeping.   *310*
Discipline must be; the scourge is deemed due.
But ah, for the sickening and strange heart-benumbing,
Compassionate abasement in shipmates that view;
Such a grand champion shamed there succumbing!

"Brown, tie him up."—The cord he brooked:
How else?—his arms spread apart—never threaping;
No, never he flinched, never sideways he looked,
Peeled to the waistband, the marble flesh creeping,
Lashed by the sleet the officious winds urge.
In function his fellows their fellowship merge—   *320*
The twain standing high—the two boatswain's mates,
Sailors of his grade, ay, and brothers of his mess.
With sharp thongs adroop the junior one awaits
The word to uplift.

                          "Untie him—so!
Submission is enough.—Man, you may go."
Then, promenading aft, brushing fat Purser Smart,
"Flog? Never meant it—hadn't any heart.
Degrade that tall fellow?"—Such, wife, was he,
Old Captain Turret, who the brave wine could stow.
Magnanimous, you think?—but what does Dick see? *330*
Apron to your eye! Why, never fell a blow,
Cheer up, old wifie, 't was a long time ago.

But where's that sore one, crabbed and severe,
Lieutenant Don Lumbago,[62] an arch scrutineer?
Call the roll to-day, would he answer—*Here!*
When the *Blixum's* fellows to quarters mustered
How he'd lurch along the lane of gun-crews clustered,
Testy as touchwood, to pry and to peer.
Jerking his sword underneath larboard arm,
He ground his worn grinders to keep himself calm.   *340*

Composed in his nerves, from the fidgets set free,
Tell, Sweet Wrinkles, alive now is he,
In Paradise a parlor where the even tempers he?

Where's Commander All-a-Tanto?
Where's Orlop Bob singing up from below?
Where's Rhyming Ned? has he spun his last canto?
Where's Jewsharp Jim? Where's Rigadoon Joe?
Ah, for the music over and done,
The band all dismissed save the droned trombone!
Where's Glen o' the gun-room, who loved Hot-
    Scotch—   *350*
Glen, prompt and cool in a perilous watch?
Where's flaxen-haired Phil? a gray lieutenant?
Or rubicund, flying a dignified pennant?
But where sleeps his brother?—the cruise it was o'er,
But ah, for death's grip that welcomed him ashore!
Where's Sid, the cadet, so frank in his brag,
Whose toast was audacious—*"Here's Sid, and Sid's
    flag!"*
Like holiday-craft that have sunk unknown,
May a lark of a lad go lonely down?
Who takes the census under the sea?   *360*
Can others like old ensigns be,
Bunting I hoisted to flutter at the gaff—
Rags in end that once were flags
Gallant streaming from the staff?
Such scurvy doom could the chances deal
To Top-Gallant Harry and Jack Genteel?

Lo, Genteel Jack in hurricane weather,
Shagged like a bear, like a red lion roaring;
But O, so fine in his chapeau and feather,
In port to the ladies never once *jawing;*   *370*
All bland *politesse,* how urbane was he—
"Oui, mademoiselle"—*"Ma chère amie!"*

'T was Jack got up the ball at Naples,
Gay in the old *Ohio* glorious;
His hair was curled by the berth-deck barber,
Never you'd deemed him a cub of rude Boreas;
In tight little pumps, with the grand dames in rout,
A-flinging his shapely foot all about;
His watch-chain with love's jeweled tokens abounding,
Curls ambrosial shaking out odors,   *380*
Waltzing along the batteries, astounding
The gunner glum and the grim-visaged loaders.

Wife, where be all these blades, I wonder,
Pennoned fine fellows, so strong, so gay?
Never their colors with a dip dived under;
Have they hauled them down in a lack-lustre day,
Or beached their boats in the Far, Far Away?

Hither and thither, blown wide asunder,
Where's this fleet, I wonder and wonder.
Slipt their cables, rattled their adieu,   *390*
(Whereaway pointing? to what rendezvous?)
Out of sight, out of mind, like the crack *Constitution,*
And many a keel time never shall renew—
Bon Homme Dick o'the buff Revolution,
The *Black Cockade* and the staunch *True-Blue.*

Doff hats to Decatur! But where is his blazon?
Must merited fame endure time's wrong—
Glory's ripe grape wizen up to a raisin?
Yes! for Nature teems,[63] and the years are strong,
And who can keep the tally o' the names that fleet
    along!   *400*

But his frigate, wife, his bride? Would blacksmiths
    brown
Into smithereens smite the solid old renown?

Riveting the bolts in the iron-clad's shell,
Hark to the hammers with a *rat-tat-tat;*
"Handier a *derby* than a laced cocked hat!
The *Monitor* was ugly, but she served us right well,
Better than the *Cumberland*, a beauty and the belle."

Better than the Cumberland!—Heart alive in me!
That battlemented hull, Tantallon o' the sea,
Kicked in, as at Boston the taxed chests o' tea!   *410*
Ay, spurned by the *ram*, once a tall, shapely craft,
But lopped by the *Rebs* to an iron-beaked raft—
A blacksmith's unicorn in armor *cap-à-pie.*

Under the water-line a *ram's* blow is dealt:
And foul fall the knuckles that strike below the belt.
Nor brave the inventions that serve to replace
The openness of valor while dismantling the grace.

Aloof from all this and the never-ending game,
Tantamount to teetering, plot and counterplot;
Impenetrable armor—all-perforating shot;   *420*
Aloof, bless God, ride the war-ships of old,
A grand fleet moored in the roadstead of fame;
Not submarine sneaks with *them* are enrolled;
Their long shadows dwarf us, their flags are as flame.

Don't fidget so, wife; an old man's passion
Amounts to no more than this smoke that I puff;
There, there, now, buss me in good old fashion;
A died-down candle will flicker in the snuff.

But one last thing let your old babbler say,
What Decatur's coxswain said who was long ago
        hearsed,   *430*
"Take in your flying-kites, for there comes a lubber's day
When gallant things will go, and the three-deckers first."

My pipe is smoked out, and the grog runs slack;
But bowse away, wife, at your blessed Bohea;
This empty can here must needs solace me—
Nay, sweetheart, nay; I take that back;
Dick drinks from your eyes and he finds no lack!

The Scout Toward Aldie

The cavalry-camp lies on the slope
  Of what was late a vernal hill,
But now like a pavement bare—
An outpost in the perilous wilds
  Which ever are lone and still;
      But Mosby's men are there—
      Of Mosby best beware.

Great trees the troopers felled, and leaned
  In antlered walls about their tents;
Strict watch they kept; 'twas *Hark!* and *Mark!*   *10*
Unarmed none cared to stir abroad
  For berries beyond their forest-fence:
      As glides in seas the shark,
      Rides Mosby through green dark.

All spake of him, but few had seen
  Except the maimed ones or the low;
Yet rumor made him every thing—
A farmer—woodman—refugee—
  The man who crossed the field but now;
      A spell about his life did cling—   *20*
      Who to the ground shall Mosby bring?

The morning-bugles lonely play,
  Lonely the evening-bugle calls—

Unanswered voices in the wild;
The settled hush of birds in nest
Becharms, and all the wood enthralls:
    Memory's self is so beguiled
    That Mosby seems a satyr's child.

They lived as in the Eerie Land—
    The fire-flies showed with fairy gleam;   30
And yet from pine-tops one might ken
The Capitol Dome—hazy—sublime—
    A vision breaking on a dream:
        So strange it was that Mosby's men
        Should dare to prowl where the Dome was seen.

A ride[64] toward Aldie broke the spell.—
    The Leader lies before his tent
Gazing at heaven's all-cheering lamp
Through blandness of a morning rare;
    His thoughts on bitter-sweets are bent: 40
        His sunny bride is in the camp—
        But Mosby—graves are beds of damp!

The trumpet calls; he goes within;
    But none the prayer and sob may know:
Her hero he, but bridegroom too.
Ah, love in a tent is a queenly thing,
    And fame, be sure, refines the vow;
        But fame fond wives have lived to rue,
        And Mosby's men fell deeds can do.

Tan-tara! tan-tara! tan-tara!   50
    Mounted and armed he sits a king;
For pride she smiles if now she peep—
Elate he rides at the head of his men;
    He is young, and command is a boyish thing:
        They file out into the forest deep—
        Do Mosby and his rangers sleep?

The sun is gold, and the world is green,
  Opal the vapors of morning roll;
The champing horses lightly prance—
Full of caprice, and the riders too   *60*
  Curving in many a caricole.
      But marshaled soon, by fours advance—
      Mosby had checked that airy dance.

By the hospital-tent the cripples stand—
  Bandage, and crutch, and cane, and sling,
And palely eye the brave array;
The froth of the cup is gone for them
  (Caw! caw! the crows through the blueness wing):
      Yet these were late as bold, as gay;
      But Mosby—a clip, and grass is hay.   *70*

How strong they feel on their horses free,
  Tingles the tendoned thigh with life;
Their cavalry jackets make boys of all—
With golden breasts like the oriole;
  The chat, the jest, and laugh are rife.
      But word is passed from the front—a call
      For order; the wood is Mosby's hall.

To which behest one rider sly
  (Spurred, but unarmed) gave little heed—
Of dexterous fun not slow or spare,   *80*
He teased his neighbors of touchy mood,
  Into plungings he pricked his steed:
      A black-eyed man on a coal-black mare,
      Alive as Mosby in mountain air.

His limbs were long, and large, and round;
  He whispered, winked—did all but shout:
A healthy man for the sick to view;
The taste in his mouth was sweet at morn;
  Little of care he cared about.

And yet of pains and pangs he knew—   *90*
In others, maimed by Mosby's crew.

The Hospital Steward—even he
(Sacred in person as a priest),
And on his coat-sleeve broidered nice
Wore the caduceus, black and green.
    No wonder he sat so light on his beast;
    This cheery man in suit of price
    Not even Mosby dared to slice.

They pass the picket by the pine
And hollow log—a dreary[65] place;   *100*
His horse adroop, and pistol clean;
'Tis cocked—kept leveled toward the wood;
    Strained vigilance ages his childish face.
    Since midnight has that stripling been
    Peering for Mosby through the green.

Splashing they cross the freshet-flood,
And up the muddy bank they strain;
A horse at a spectral white-ash shies—
One of the span of the ambulance,
    Black as a hearse. They give the rein: *110*
    Silent speed on a scout were wise,
    Could cunning baffle Mosby's spies.

Rumor had come that a band was lodged
In green retreats of hills that peer
By Aldie (famed for the swordless charge).[66]
Much store they'd heaped of captured arms
    And, peradventure, pilfered cheer;
    For Mosby's lads oft hearts enlarge
    In revelry by some gorge's marge.

"Don't let your sabres rattle and ring;   *120*
To his oat-bag let each man give heed—

There now, that fellow's bag's untied,
Sowing the road with the precious grain.
   Your carbines swing at hand—you need!
      Look to yourselves, and your nags beside,
      Men who after Mosby ride."

Picked lads and keen went sharp before—
   A guard, though scarce against surprise;
And rearmost rode an answering troop,
But flankers none to right or left.   *130*
   No bugle peals, no pennon flies:
      Silent they sweep, and fain would swoop
      On Mosby with an Indian whoop.

On, right on through the forest land,
   Nor man, nor maid, nor child was seen—
Not even a dog. The air was still;
The blackened hut they turned to see,
   And spied charred benches on the green;
      A squirrel sprang from the rotting mill
      Whench Mosby sallied late, brave blood to
         spill.   *140*

By worn-out fields they cantered on—
   Drear fields amid the woodlands wide;
By cross-roads of some olden time,
In which grew groves; by gate-stones down—
   Grassed ruins of secluded pride:
      A spell-bound land,[67] long past the prime,
      Fit land for Mosby or for crime.

The brook in the dell they pass. One peers
   Between the leaves: "Ay, there's the place—
There, on the oozy ledge—'twas there   *150*
We found the body (Blake's, you know);
   Such whirlings, gurglings round the face—

Shot drinking! Well, in war all's fair—
So Mosby says. The bough—take care!"

Hard by, a chapel. Flower-pot mould
   Danked and decayed the shaded roof;
The porch was punk; the clapboards spanned
With ruffled lichens gray or green;
   Red coral-moss was not aloof;
      And mid dry leaves green dead-man's-hand   *160*
      Groped toward that chapel in Mosby-land.

The road they leave[68] and take the wood,
   And mark the trace of ridges there—
A wood where once had slept the farm—
A wood where once tobacco grew
   Drowsily in the hazy air,
      And wrought in all kind things a calm—
      Such influence, Mosby! bids disarm.

To ease even yet the place did woo—
   To ease which pines unstirring share,   *170*
For ease the weary horses sighed:
Halting, and slackening girths, they feed,
   Their pipes they light, they loiter there;
      Then up, and urging still the Guide,
      On, and after Mosby ride.

This Guide in frowzy coat of brown,
   And beard of ancient growth and mould,
Bestrode a bony steed and strong,
As suited well with bulk he bore—
   A wheezy man with depth of hold   *180*
      Who jouncing went. A staff he swung—
      A wight whom Mosby's wasp had stung.

Burnt out and homeless—hunted long!

That wheeze he caught in autumn-wood
Crouching (a fat man) for his life,
And spied his lean son 'mong the crew
That probed the covert. Ah! black blood
    Was his 'gainst even child and wife—
    Fast friends to Mosby. Such the strife.

A lad, unhorsed by sliding girths,   *190*
    Strains hard to readjust his seat
Ere the main body show the gap
'Twixt them and the rear-guard; scrub-oaks near
He sidelong eyes, while hands move fleet;
    Then mounts and spurs. One drops his cap—
    "Let Mosby find!" nor heeds mishap.

A gable time-stained peeps through trees:
    "You mind the fight in the haunted house?
That's it; we clenched them in the room—
An ambuscade of ghosts, we deemed,[69]   *200*
    But proved sly rebels on a bouse!
    Luke lies in the yard." The chimneys loom:
    Some muse on Mosby—some on doom.

Less nimbly now through brakes they wind,
    And ford wild creeks where men have drowned;
The pool they skirt,[70] avoid the fen,
And so till night, when down they lie,
    Their steeds still saddled, in wooded ground:
    Rein in hand they slumber then,
    Dreaming of Mosby's cedarn den.   *210*

But Colonel and Major friendly sat
    Where boughs deformed low made a seat.
The Young Man talked (all sworded and spurred)
Of the partisan's blade he longed to win,
    And frays in which he meant to beat.
    The grizzled Major smoked, and heard:

"But what's that—Mosby?" "No, a bird."

A contrast here like sire and son,
   Hope and Experience sage did meet;
The Youth was brave, the Senior too;   *220*
But through the Seven Days one had served,
   And gasped with the rear-guard in retreat:
      So he smoked and smoked, and the wreath he
        blew—
      "Any *sure* news of Mosby's crew?"

He smoked and smoked, eyeing the while
   A huge tree hydra-like in growth—
Moon-tinged—with crook'd boughs rent or lopped—
Itself a haggard forest. "Come!"
   The Colonel cried, "to talk you're loath;
      D'ye hear? I say he must be stopped,   *230*
      This Mosby—caged, and hair close cropped."

"Of course; but what's that dangling there?"
   "Where?" "From the tree—that gallows-bough;"
"A bit of frayed bark, is it not?"
"Ay—or a rope; did *we* hang last?—
   Don't like my neckerchief any how;"
      He loosened it: "O ay, we'll stop
      This Mosby—but that vile jerk and drop!"[71]

By peep of light they feed and ride,
   Gaining a grove's green edge at morn,   *240*
And mark the Aldie hills uprear
And five gigantic horsemen carved
   Clear-cut against the sky withdrawn;
      Are more behind? an open snare?
      Or Mosby's men but watchmen there?

The ravaged land was miles behind,
   And Loudon spread her landscape rare;

Orchards in pleasant lowlands stood,
Cows were feeding, a cock loud crew,
But not a friend at need was there;   *250*
The valley-folk were only good
To Mosby and his wandering brood.

What best to do? what mean yon men?
Colonel and Guide their minds compare;
Be sure some looked their Leader through;
Dismounted, on his sword he leaned
As one who feigns an easy air;
And yet perplexed he was they knew—
Perplexed by Mosby's mountain-crew.

The Major hemmed as he would speak,   *260*
But checked himself, and left the ring
Of cavalrymen about their Chief—
Young courtiers mute who paid their court
By looking with confidence on their king;
They knew him brave, foresaw no grief—
But Mosby—the time for thought is brief.

The Surgeon (sashed in sacred green)
Was glad 'twas not for *him* to say
What next should be; if a trooper bleeds,
Why he will do his best, as wont,   *270*
And his partner in black will aid and pray;
But judgment bides with him who leads,
And Mosby many a problem breeds.

This Surgeon was the kindliest man
That ever a callous trade professed;
He felt for him, that Leader young,
And offered medicine from his flask:
The Colonel took it with marvelous zest.
For such fine medicine good and strong,
Oft Mosby and his foresters long.   *280*

A charm of proof. "Ho, Major, come—
  Pounce on yon men! Take half your troop,
Through the thickets wind—pray speedy be—
And gain their rear. And, Captain Morn,
  Picket these roads—all travelers stop;
    The rest to the edge of this crest with me,
    That Mosby and his scouts may see."

Commanded and done. Ere the sun stood steep,
  Back came the Blues, with a troop of Grays,
Ten riding double—luckless ten!—   *290*
Five horses gone, and looped hats lost,
  And love-locks dancing in a maze—
    Certes, but sophomores from the glen
    Of Mosby—not his veteran men.

"Colonel," said the Major, touching his cap,
  "We've had our ride, and here they are."
"Well done! how many found you there?"
  "As many as I bring you here."
    "And no one hurt?" "There'll be no scar—
    One fool was battered." "Find their lair?" *300*
    "Why, Mosby's brood camp every where."

He sighed, and slid down from his horse,
  And limping went to a spring-head nigh.
"Why, bless me, Major, not hurt, I hope?"
"Battered my knee against a bar
  When the rush was made; all right by-and-by.—
    Halloa! they gave you too much rope—
    Go back to Mosby, eh? elope?"

Just by the low-hanging skirt of wood
  The guard, remiss, had given a chance   *310*
For a sudden sally into the cover—
But foiled the intent, nor fired a shot,
  Though the issue was a deadly trance;

> For, hurled 'gainst an oak that humped low over,
> Mosby's man fell, pale as a lover.

They pulled some grass his head to ease
  (Lined with blue shreds a ground-nest stirred).
The Surgeon came—"Here's a to-do!"
"Ah!" cried the Major, darting a glance,
  "This fellow's the one that fired and spurred   *320*
    Down hill, but met reserves below—
    My boys, not Mosby's—so we go!"

The Surgeon—bluff, red, goodly man—
  Kneeled by the hurt one; like a bee
He toiled. The pale young Chaplain too—
  (Who went to the wars for cure of souls,
    And his own student-ailments)—he
    Bent over likewise; spite the two
    Mosby's poor man more pallid grew.

Meanwhile the mounted captives near   *330*
  Jested; and yet they anxious showed;
Virginians; some of family-pride,
And young, and full of fire, and fine
  In open feature and cheek that glowed;
    And here thralled vagabonds now they ride—
    But list! one speaks for Mosby's side.

"Why, three to one—your horses strong—
  Revolvers, rifles, and a surprise—
Surrender we account no shame!
We live, are gay, and life is hope;   *340*
  We'll fight again when fight is wise.
    There are plenty more from where we came;
    But go find Mosby—start the game!"

Yet one there was who looked but glum;

In middle-age, a father he,
And this his first experience too:
"They shot at my heart when my hands were up—
    This fighting's crazy work, I see!"
    But noon is high; what next to do?
    The woods are mute, and Mosby is the foe.   *350*

"Save what we've got," the Major said;
    "Bad plan to make a scout too long;
The tide may turn, and drag them back,
And more beside. These rides I've been,
    And every time a mine was sprung.
    To rescue, mind, they won't be slack—
    Look out for Mosby's rifle-crack."

"We'll welcome it! give crack for crack!
    Peril, old lad, is what I seek."
"O then, there's plenty to be had—   *360*
By all means on, and have our fill!"
    With that, grotesque, he writhed his neck,
    Showing a scar by buck-shot made—
    Kind Mosby's Christmas gift, he said.

"But, Colonel, my prisoners—let a guard
    Make sure of them, and lead to camp.
That done, we're free for a dark-room fight
If so you say." The other laughed;
    "Trust me, Major, nor throw a damp.
    But first to try a little sleight—   *370*
    Sure news of Mosby would suit me quite."

Herewith he turned—"Reb, have a dram?"
    Holding the Surgeon's flask with a smile
To a young scapegrace from the glen.
"O yes!" he eagerly replied,
    "And thank you, Colonel, but—any guile?

For if you think we'll blab—why, then
You don't know Mosby or his men."

The Leader's genial air relaxed.
  "Best give it up," a whisperer said.   *380*
"By heaven, I'll range their rebel den!"
"They'll treat you well," the captive cried;
  "They're all like us—handsome—well bred;
    In wood or town, with sword or pen,
    Polite is Mosby, bland his men."

"Where were you, lads, last night?—come, tell!"
  "We?—at a wedding in the Vale—
The bridegroom our comrade; by his side
Belisent, my cousin—O, so proud
  Of her young love with old wounds pale—   *390*
    A Virginian girl! God bless her pride—
    Of a crippled Mosby-man the bride!"

"Four walls shall mend that saucy mood,
  And moping prisons tame him down,"
Said Captain Cloud. "God help that day,"
Cried Captain Morn, "and he so young.
  But hark, he sings—a madcap one!"
    "O we multiply merrily in the May,
    The birds and Mosby's men, they say!"

While echoes ran, a wagon old,   *400*
  Under stout guard of Corporal Chew
Came up; a lame horse, dingy white,
With clouted harness; ropes in hand,
  Cringed the humped driver, black in hue;
    By him (for Mosby's band a sight)
    A sister-rebel sat, her veil held tight.

"I picked them up," the Corporal said,

"Crunching their way over stick and root,
Through yonder wood. The man here—Cuff—
Says they are going to Leesburg town."   *410*
    The Colonel's eye took in the group;
        The veiled one's hand he spied—enough!
        Not Mosby's. Spite the gown's poor stuff,

Off went his hat: "Lady, fear not;
    We soldiers do what we deplore—
I must detain you till we march."
    The stranger nodded. Nettled now,
        He grew politer than before:—
        "'Tis Mosby's fault, this halt and search."
        The lady stiffened in her starch.   *420*

"My duty, madam, bids me now
    Ask what may seem a little rude.
Pardon—that veil—withdraw it, please
(Corporal! make every man fall back);
    Pray, now, I do but what I should;
        Bethink you, 'tis in masks like these
        That Mosby haunts the villages."

Slowly the stranger drew her veil,
    And looked the Soldier in the eye—
A glance of mingled foul and fair;   *430*
Sad patience in a proud disdain,
    And more than quietude. A sigh
        She heaved, as if all unaware,
        And far seemed Mosby from her care.

She came from Yewton Place, her home,
    So ravaged by the war's wild play—
Campings, and foragings, and fires—
That now she sought an aunt's abode.
    Her kinsmen? In Lee's army, they.

The black? A servant, late her sire's.   *440*
And Mosby? Vainly he inquires.

He gazed, and sad she met his eye;
  "In the wood yonder were you lost?"
No; at the forks they left the road
Because of hoof-prints (thick they were—
    Thick as the words in notes thrice crossed),
      And fearful, made that episode.
      In fear of Mosby? None she showed.

Her poor attire again he scanned:
  "Lady, once more; I grieve to jar   *450*
On all sweet usage, but must plead
To have what peeps there from your dress;
    That letter—'tis justly prize of war."
      She started—gave it—she must need.
      "'Tis not from Mosby? May I read?"

And straight such matter he perused
  That with the Guide he went apart.
The Hospital Steward's turn began:
"Must squeeze this darkey; every tap
    Of knowledge we are bound to start."   *460*
      "Garry," she said, "tell all you can
      Of Colonel Mosby—that brave man."

"Dun know much, sare; and missis here
  Know less dan me. But dis I know—"
"Well, what?" "I dun know what I know."
"A knowing answer!" The hump-back coughed,
  Rubbing his yellowish wool like tow.
      "Come—Mosby—tell!" "O dun look so!
      My gal nursed missis—let we go."

"Go where?" demanded Captain Cloud;   *470*

"Back into bondage? Man, you're free!"
"Well, *let* we free!" The Captain's brow
Lowered; the Colonel came—had heard:
  "Pooh! pooh! his simple heart I see—
    A faithful servant.—Lady" (a bow),
    "Mosby's abroad—with us you'll go.

"Guard! look to your prisoners; back to camp!
  The man in the grass—can he mount and away?
Why, how he groans!" "Bad inward bruise—
Might lug him along in the ambulance."   *480*
  "Coals to Newcastle! let him stay.
    Boots and saddles!—our pains we lose,
    Nor care I if Mosby hear the news!"

But word was sent to a house at hand,
  And a flask was left by the hurt one's side.
They seized in that same house a man,
Neutral by day, by night a foe—
  So charged his neighbor late, the Guide.
    A grudge? Hate will do what it can;
    Along he went for a Mosby-man.   *490*

No secrets now; the bugle calls;
  The open road they take, nor shun
The hill; retrace the weary way.
But one there was who whispered low,
  "This is a feint—we'll back anon;
    Young Hair-Brains don't retreat, they say;
    A brush with Mosby is the play!"

They rode till eve. Then on a farm
  That lay along a hill-side green,
Bivouacked. Fires were made, and then   *500*
Coffee was boiled; a cow was coaxed
  And killed, and savory roasts were seen;

And under the lee of a cattle-pen
The guard supped freely with Mosby's men.

The ball was bandied to and fro;
　　Hits were given and hits were met:
"Chickamauga, Feds—take off your hat!"
"But the Fight in the Clouds repaid you, Rebs!"
　　"Forgotten about Manassas yet?"
　　　　Chatting and chaffing, and tit for tat,　　　*510*
　　　　Mosby's clan with the troopers sat.

"Here comes the moon!" a captive cried;
　　"A song." what say? Archy, my lad!"
Hailing the still one of the clan
(A boyish face with girlish hair),
　　"Give us that thing poor Pansy made
　　　　Last year." He brightened, and began;
　　　　And this was the song of Mosby's man:

　　　　Spring is come; she shows her pass—
　　　　　　Wild violets cool!　　　　　　　*520*
　　　　South of woods a small close grass—
　　　　　　A vernal wool!
　　　　Leaves are a'bud on the sassafras—
　　　　　　They'll soon be full:
　　　　Blessings on the friendly screen—
　　　　I'm for the South! says the leafage green.

　　　　Robins! fly, and take your fill
　　　　　　Of out-of-doors—
　　　　Garden, orchard, meadow, hill,
　　　　　　Barns and bowers;　　　　　　　*530*
　　　　Take your fill, and have your will—
　　　　　　Virginia's yours!
　　　　But, bluebirds! keep away, and fear

The ambuscade in bushes here.

"A green song that," a sergeant said;
  "But where's poor Pansy? gone, I fear."
"Ay, mustered out at Ashby's Gap."
"I see; now for a live man's song;
  Ditty for ditty—prepare to cheer.
    Comrades,[72] you can fling a cap!   *540*
    You barehead Mosby-boys—why—clap!"

> *Nine Blue-coats went a-nutting*
>   *Slyly in Tennessee—*
> *Not for chestnuts—better than that—*
>   *Hush, you bumble-bee!*
>   *Nutting, nutting—*
>   *All through the year there's nutting!*

> *A tree they spied so yellow,*
>   *Rustling in motion queer;*
> *In they fired, and down they dropped—*   *550*
>   *Butternuts, my dear!*
>   *Nutting, nutting—*
>   *Who'll 'list to go a-nutting?*

Ah! why should good fellows foemen be?
  And who would dream that foes they were—
Larking and singing so friendly then—
A family likeness in every face.
  But Captain Cloud made sour demur:
    "Guard! keep your prisoners *in* the pen,
    And let none talk with Mosby's men."   *560*

That captain was a valorous one
  (No irony, but honest truth),
Yet down from his brain cold drops distilled,

Making stalactites in his heart—
　A conscientious soul, forsooth;
　　　And with a formal hate was filled
　　　Of Mosby's band; and some he'd killed.

Meantime the lady rueful sat,
　Watching the flicker of a fire
Where the Colonel played the outdoor host　　　*570*
In brave old hall of ancient Night.
　But ever the dame grew shyer and shyer,
　　　Seeming with private grief engrossed—
　　　Grief far from Mosby, housed or lost.

The ruddy embers showed her pale.
　The Soldier did his best devoir:
"Some coffee?—no?—a cracker?—one?"
Cared for her servant—sought to cheer:
　"I know, I know—a cruel war!
　　　But wait—even Mosby'll eat his bun;　　　*580*
　　　The Old Hearth—back to it anon!"

But cordial words no balm could bring;
　She sighed, and kept her inward chafe,
And seemed to hate the voice of glee—
Joyless and tearless. Soon he called
　An escort: "See this lady safe
　　　In yonder house.—Madam, you're free.
　　　And now for Mosby.—Guide! with me."

("A night-ride, eh") "Tighten your girths!
　But, buglers! not a note from you.　　　*590*
Fling more rails on the fires—a blaze!"
("Sergeant, a feint—I told you so—
　Toward Aldie again. Bivouac, adieu!")
　　　After the cheery flames they gaze,
　　　Then back for Mosby through the maze.

The moon looked through the trees, and tipped
  The scabbards with her elfin beam;
The Leader backward cast his glance,
Proud of the cavalcade that came—
  A hundred horses, bay and cream: *600*
    "Major! look how the lads advance—
    Mosby we'll have in the ambulance!"

"No doubt, no doubt:—was that a hare?—
  First catch, then cook; and cook him brown."
"Trust me to catch," the other cried—
"The lady's letter!—a dance, man, dance
  This night is given in Leesburg town!"
      "He'll be there, too!" wheezed out the Guide;
      "That Mosby loves a dance and ride!"

"The lady, ah!—the lady's letter—   *610*
  A *lady,* then, is in the case,"
Muttered the Major. "Ay, her aunt
  Writes her to come by Friday eve
  (To-night), for people of the place,
      At Mosby's last fight jubilant,
      A party give, though table-cheer be scant."

The Major hemmed. "Then this night-ride
  We owe to her?—One lighted house
In a town else dark.—The moths, begar!
Are not quite yet all dead!" "How? how?"   *620*
  "A mute, meek, mournful little mouse!—
      Mosby has wiles which subtle are—

      But woman's wiles in wiles of war!"
"Tut, Major! by what craft or guile—"
  "Can't tell! but he'll be found in wait.
Softly we enter, say, the town—
Good! pickets post, and all so sure—
      When—crack! the rifles from every gate,

The Gray-backs fire—dash up and down—
Each alley unto Mosby's known!"   *630*

"Now, Major, now—you take dark views
    Of a moonlight night." "Well, well, we'll see,"
And smoked as if each whiff were gain.
The other mused; then sudden asked,
    "What would you do in grand decree?"
        "I'd beat, if I could, Lee's armies—then
        Send constables after Mosby's men."

"Ay, ay!—you're odd." The moon sailed up;
    On through the shadowy land they went.
"Names must be made and printed be!"   *640*
Hummed the blithe Colonel. "Doc, your flask!
    Major, I drink to your good content.
        My pipe is out—enough for me!
        This gold-lace gleams[73]—does Mosby see?

"But what comes here?" A man from the front
    Reported a tree athwart the road.
"Go round it, then; no time to bide;
All right—go on! Were one to stay
    For each distrust of a nervous mood,
        Long miles we'd make in this our ride   *650*
        Through Mosby-land.—On! with the Guide!"

Then sportful to the Surgeon turned:
    "Green sashes hardly serve by night!"
"Nor bullets nor bottles," the Major sighed,
"Against these moccasin-snakes—such foes
    As seldom come to solid fight:
        They kill and vanish; through grass they glide;
        Devil take Mosby!"—his horse here shied.

"Hold! look—the tree, like a dragged balloon;

A globe of leaves—some trickery here;   *660*
My nag is right—best now be shy."
A movement was made, a hubbub and snarl;
    Little was plain—they blindly steer.
        The Pleiads, as from ambush sly,
        Peep out—Mosby's men in the sky!

As restive they turn, how sore they feel,
    And cross, and sleepy, and full of spleen,
And curse the war. "Fools, North and South!"
Said one right out. "O for a bed!
    O now to drop in this woodland green!"   *670*
        He drops as the syllables leave his mouth—
        Mosby speaks from the undergrowth—

Speaks in a volley! out jets the flame!
    Men fall from their saddles like plums from trees;
Horses take fright, reins tangle and bind;
"Steady—dismount—form—and into the wood!"
    They go, but find what scarce can please:
        Their steeds have been tied in the field behind,
        And Mosby's men are off like the wind.

Sound the recall! vain to pursue—   *680*
    The enemy scatters in wilds he knows,
To reunite in his own good time;
And, to follow, they need divide—
    To come astray[74] on crouching foes:
        Maple and hemlock, beech and lime,
        Are Mosby's confederates, share the crime.

"Major," burst in a bugler small,
    "The fellow we left in Loudon grass—
Sir Slyboots with the inward bruise,
His voice I heard—the very same—   *690*
    Some watchword in the ambush pass;

Ay, sir, we had him in his shoes—
We caught him—Mosby—but to lose!"

"Go, go!—these saddle-dreamers! Well,
    And here's another.—Cool, sir, cool!"
"Major, I saw them mount and sweep,
And one was humped,[75] or I mistake,
    And in the skurry dropped his wool."
        "A wig! go fetch it:—the lads need sleep;
        They'll next see Mosby in a sheep!   *700*

"Come, come, fall back! reform your ranks—
    All's jackstraws here! Where's Captain Morn?—
We've parted like boats in a raging tide!
But stay—the Colonel—did he charge?
    And comes he there? 'Tis streak of dawn;
        Mosby is off, the woods are wide—
        Hist! there's a groan—this crazy ride!"

As they searched for the fallen, the dawn grew chill;
    They lay in the dew: "Ah, hurt much, Mink?
And—yes—the Colonel!" Dead! but so calm   *710*
That death seemed nothing—even death,
    The thing we deem every thing heart can think;
        Amid wilding roses that shed their balm,
        Careless of Mosby he lay—in a charm!

The Major took him by the hand—
    Into the friendly clasp it bled
(A ball through heart and hand he rued):
"Good-bye!" and gazed with humid glance;
    Then in a hollow revery said,
        "The weakest thing is lustihood;   *720*
        But Mosby"—and he checked his mood.

"Where's the advance?—cut off, by heaven!

Come, Surgeon, how with your wounded there?"
"The ambulance will carry all."
"Well, get them in; we go to camp.
   Seven prisoners gone? for the rest have care."
      Then to himself, "This grief is gall;
      That Mosby!—I'll cast a silver ball!"

"Ho!" turning—"Captain Cloud, you mind
   The place where the escort went—so shady?   *730*
Go, search every closet low and high,
And barn, and bin, and hidden bower—
   Every covert—find that lady!
      And yet I may misjudge her—ay,
      Women (like Mosby) mystify.

"We'll see. Ay, Captain, go—with speed!
   Surround and search; each living thing
Secure; that done, await us where
We last turned off. Stay! fire the cage
   If the birds be flown." By the cross-road spring   *740*
      The bands rejoined; no words; the glare
      Told all. Had Mosby plotted there?

The weary troop that wended now—
   Hardly it seemed the same that pricked
Forth to the forest from the camp:
Foot-sore horses, jaded men;
   Every backbone felt as nicked,
      Each eye dim as a sick-room lamp,
      All faces stamped with Mosby's stamp.

In order due the Major rode—   *750*
   Chaplain and Surgeon on either hand;
A riderless horse a negro led;
In a wagon the blanketed sleeper went;
   Then the ambulance with the bleeding band;

And, an emptied oat-bag on each head,
Went Mosby's men, and marked the dead.

What gloomed them? what so cast them down,
    And changed the cheer that late they took,
As double-guarded now they rode
Between the files of moody men?   *760*
    Some sudden consciousness they brook,
        Or dread the sequel. That night's blood
        Disturbed even Mosby's brotherhood.

The flagging horses stumbled at roots,
    Floundered in mires, or clinked the stones;
No rider spake except aside;
But the wounded cramped in the ambulance,
    It was horror to hear their groans—
        Jerked along in the woodland ride,
        While Mosby's clan their revery hide.   *770*

The Hospital Steward—even he—
    Who on the sleeper kept his glance,
Was changed; late bright-black beard and eye
Looked now hearse-black; his heavy heart,
    Like his fagged mare, no more could dance;
        His grape was now a raisin dry:
        'Tis Mosby's homily—*Man must die.*

The amber sunset flushed the camp
    As on the hill their eyes they fed;
The pickets dumb looks at the wagon dart;   *780*
A handkerchief waves from the bannered tent—
    As white, alas! the face of the dead:
        Who shall the withering news impart?
        The bullet of Mosby goes through heart to heart!

They buried him where the lone ones lie

(Lone sentries shot on midnight post)—
A green-wood grave-yard hid from ken,
Where sweet-fern flings an odor nigh—
    Yet held in fear for the gleaming ghost!
        Though the bride should see threescore and
          ten,   *790*
        She will dream of Mosby and his men.

How halt the verse, and turn aside—
    The cypress falls athwart the way;
No joy remains for bard to sing;
And heaviest dole of all is this,
    That other hearts shall be as gay
        As hers that now no more shall spring:
        To Mosby-land the dirges cling.

Marquis De Grandvin

Be Borgia Pope, be Bomba King,
The roses blow, the song-birds sing.[76]

AT THE HOSTELRY

Not wanting in the traditional suavity of his country-
men, the Marquis makes his salutation. Thereafter, with
an ulterior design, entering upon a running retrospect
touching Italian affairs.

> Candid eyes in open faces
> Clear, not keen, no narrowing line:
> Hither turn your favoring graces
> Now the cloth is drawn for wine.

In best of worlds if all's not bright,
Allow, the shadow's chased by light,
Though rest for neither yet may be.
And beauty's charm, where Nature reigns,
Nor crimes nor codes may quite subdue,
As witness Naples long in chains   *10*
Exposed dishevelled by the sea—
Ah, so much more her beauty drew,
Till Savoy's red-shirt Perseus flew
And cut that fair Andromeda free.

There[77] Fancy flies. Nor less the trite
Matter-of-fact transcends the flight:
A rail-way train took Naples town;
But Garibaldi sped thereon:
This movement's rush sufficing there
To rout King Fanny, Bomba's heir,   *20*
Already stuffing trunks and hampers,
At news that from Sicilia passed—
The banished Bullock from the Pampas
Trampling the royal levies massed.

And, later: *He has swum the Strait,*
And in Calabria making head,
Cheered by the peasants garlanded,
Pushes for Naples' nearest gate.
From that red Taurus plunging on
With lowered horns and forehead dun,   *30*
Shall matadores save Bomba's son?
He fled. And her Redeemer's banners
Glad Naples greeted with strewn flowers,
Hurrahs, and secular hosannas
That fidgety made all tyrant powers.

Ye halls of history, arched by time,
Founded in fate, enlarged by crime,
Now shines like phosphorus scratched in dark
'Gainst your grimed walls the luminous mark
Of one who in no paladin age   *40*
Was knightly—him who lends a page
Now signal in time's recent story
Where scarce in vogue are "Plutarch's Men,"
And jobbers deal in popular glory.—
But he the hero was a sword
Whereto at whiles Cavour was guard.
The point described a fiery arc,
A swerve of wrist ordained the mark.

Wise statesmanship, a ruling star,
Made peace itself subserve the war.   *50*

In forging into fact a dream—
For dream it was, a dream for long—
Italia disenthralled and one,
Above her but the Alps—no thong
High flourished, held by Don or Hun;
Italia, how cut up, divided
Nigh paralysed, by cowls misguided;
Locked as in Chancery's numbing hand,
Fattening the predatory band
Of shyster-princes, whose ill sway   *60*
Still kept her a calamitous land;
In ending this, spite cruel delay,
And making, in the People's name,
Of Italy's disunited frame,
A unit and a telling State
Participant in the world's debate;
Few deeds of arms, in fruitful end,
The statecraft of Cavour transcend.

What towns with alien guards that teemed
Attest Art's Holy Land redeemed.   *70*

Slipt from the Grand Duke's gouty tread,
Florence, fair flower, up-lifts the head.
Ancona, plucked from Peter's Chair,
With all the Papal fiefs in band,
Her Arch Imperial now may wear[78]
For popular triumph and command.
And Venice: there the Croatian horde
Swagger no more with clattering sword,
Ruffling the doves that dot the Square.
In Rome no furtive cloaked one now   *80*
Scribbles his gibe on Pasquin's brow,

Since wag his tongue at Popes who may
The Popedom needs endure his say.
But (happier)[79] feuds with princelings cease,
The *People* federate a peace.
Cremona fiddles, blithe to see
Contentious cities comrades free.
Sicilia—Umbria—muster in
Their towns in squads, and hail Turin.
One state, one flag, one sword, one crown,   *90*
Till time build higher or Cade pull down.

Counts this for much? Well, more is won.
Brave public works are schemed or done.
Swart Tiber, dredged, may rich repay—
The Pontine Marsh, too, drained away,
And, far along the Tuscan shore
The weird Maremma reassume
Her ancient tilth and wheaten plume.
Ay, to reclaim Ansonia's land
The Spirit o' the Age he'll take a hand.   *100*
He means to dust each bric-à-brac city,
Pluck the feathers from all banditti;
The Pope he'll hat, and, yea or nay ye,
Rejuvenate e'en[80] poor old Pompeii!
Concede, accomplished aims unite
With many a promise[81] hopeful and as bright.

II

Effecting a counterturn, the Marquis evokes—and
from the Shades, as would seem—an inconclusive debate
as to the exact import of a current term significant of
that one of the manifold aspects of life and nature which
under various forms all artists strive to transmit to can-
vas. A term, be it added, whereof the lexicons give
definitions more lexicographical than satisfactory.

Ay. But the *Picturesque,* I wonder—
The *Picturesque* and *Old Romance!*
May these conform and share advance
With Italy and the world's career?   *110*
At little suppers, where I'm one,
My artist-friends this question ponder
When ale goes round; but, in brave cheer
The vineyards yield, they'll beading run
Like Arethusa burst from ground.
Ay, and in lateral freaks of gamesome wit
Moribund Old Romance irreverent twit.
"Adieu, rosettes!" sighs Steen in way
Of fun convivial, frankly gay,
"Adieu, rosettes and point-de-vise!"   *120*
All garnish strenuous time refuse;
In peacocks' tails put out the eyes!
Utility reigns[82]—Ah, well-a-way!—
And bustles along in Bentham's shoes.
For the Picturesque—suffice, suffice
The picture that fetches a picturesque price!

Less jovial ones propound at start
Your Picturesque in what inheres?
"In nature point, in life, in art
Where the essential thing appears.   *130*
First settle that, we'll then take up
The prior question."
                            "Well, so be,"
Said Frater Lippi, who but he—
Exchanging late in changeable weather
The cowl for the cap, a cap and feather;
With wicked eye then twinkling fun,
Suppressed in friendly, decorous tone,
"Here's Spagnoletto. He, I trow,
Can best avail here, and bestead.—
Come then, hidalgo, what sayst thou?   *140*

The *Picturesque*—an example yield."
The man invoked, a man of brawn
Tho' stumpt in stature, raised his head
From sombre musings, and revealed
A brow by no blest angel sealed,
And mouth at corners droopt and drawn;
And, catching but the last words, said:
"The Picturesque?—Have ye not seen
My Flaying of St. Batholomew—
My Laurence on the gridiron lean?   *150*
There's Picturesque; and done as well
As old Giotto's *Damned in Hell*
At Pisa in the Campo Santa."
They turn hereat. In merriment
Ironic jeers the juniors vent,
"That's modest now, one hates a vaunter."
But Lippi: "Why not Guido cite
In *Herod's Massacre?*"—weening well
The Little Spaniard's envious spite
Guido against, as gossips tell,   *160*
The sombrous one igniting here
And piercing Lippi's mannered mien
Flared up volcanic.—Ah, too clear,
At odds are furious and serene.

Misliking Lippi's mischievous eye
As much as Spagnoletto's mood,
And thinking to put unpleasantness by,
Swanevelt spake, that Dutchman good:
"Friends, but the Don errs not so wide.
Like beauty strange with horror allied,—   *170*
As shown in great Leonardo's head
Of snaky Medusa,—so as well
Grace and the Picturesque may dwell
With Terror. Vain here to divide—
The Picturesque has many a side.

For me, I take to Nature's scene
Some scene select, set off serene
With any tranquil thing you please—
A crumbling tower, a shepherd piping.
My master, sure, with this agrees,"   *180*
His turned appeal on Claude here lighting.
But he, the mildest tempered swain
And eke discreetest, too, may be,
That ever came out from Lorraine
To lose himself in Arcady
(Sweet there to be lost, as some have been,
And find oneself in losing e'en)
To Claude no pastime, none, nor gain
Wavering in theory's wildering maze;   *190*
Better he likes, though sunny he,
To haunt the Arcadian woods in haze,
Intent shy charms[83] to win or ensnare,
Beauty his Daphne, he the pursuer there.

So naught he said whate'er he felt,
Yet friendly nodded to Swanevelt.

III

  With all the ease of a Prince of the Blood gallantly
testifying in behalf of an indiscreet lady, the Marquis
incontinently fibs, laying the cornerstone of a Munchau-
sen fable—

But you, ye pleasant faces wise
Saluted late, your candid eyes
Methinks ye rub them in surprise:
"What's this? Jan Steen and Lippi? Claude?
Long since they embarked for Far Abroad!   *200*
Have met them, you?"
                              "Indeed, have I!

Ma foi! The immortals never die;
They are not so weak, they are not so craven;
They keep time's sea and skip the haven."—
Well, letting minor memories go:
With other illustrious ones in row
I met them once at that brave tavern
Founded by the first Delmonico,
Forefather of a flourishing line!
'Twas all in off-hand easy way—   *210*
Pour passer le temps, as loungers say.
In upper chamber did we sit
The dolts below never dreaming it.
The cloth was drawn—we left alone,
No solemn lackeys looking on.
In wine's meridian, halcyon noon,
Beatitude excludes elation.

Thus for a while. Anon ensues
All round their horizon, ruddying it,
Such Lights Auroral, mirth and wit—   *220*
Thy flashes, O Falernian Muse!

IV

    After a little by-scene between Van Dyke and Franz
Hals of Mechlin, an old topic is by the company, here
and there, discussed anew. In which rambling talk Adrian
Brouwer, tickled undesignedly[84] by two chance-words
from a certain grandee of artists, and more waggish than
polite in addressing Carlo Dolce and Rembrandt, whim-
sically delivers his mind.

'Twas Hals began. He to Van Dyke,
In whose well-polished gentle mien
The practiced courtier of Kings was seen:
"Van, how, pray, do these revels strike?

Once you'd have me to England—there
Riches to get at St. James's. Nay—
Patronage! 'Gainst that flattering snare,
The more if[85] it lure from hearth away,
Old friends—old vintages carry the day!"   *230*
Whereto Van Dyke, in silken dress
Not smoother than his courteousness,
Smiled back, "Well, Franz, go then thy ways;
Thy pencil anywhere earns thee praise,
If not heapt gold.—But hark, the chat!"
" 'Tis gay," said Hals, not deaf to that,
"And witty should be. O the cup,
Wit rises in exhalation up!"
And sympathetic viewed the scene.
Then, turning, with yet livelier mien,   *240*
"More candid than kings, less coy than the Graces,
The pleasantness, Van, of these[86] festival faces!—
But what's the theme?"
                              "The theme was bent—
Be sure, in no dry argument—
On the Picturesque, what 'tis,—its essence,
Fibre and root, bud, efflorescence,
Congenial soil, and where at best;
Till, drawing attention from the rest,
Some syllables dropt from Tintoretto,
Negligent dropt; with limp, lax air,   *250*
One long arm lolling over chair,
Nor less evincing latent nerve
Potential lazing in reserve.
For strong he was—the dyer's son,
A leonine strength, no strained falsetto—
The Little Tinto, Tintoretto,
Yes, Titan work by him was done.
And now as one in Art's degree
Superior to his topic—he:
"This *Picturesque* is scarce my care.   *260*
But note it now in Nature's work—

A thatched hut settling, rotting trees
Mossed over. Some decay must lurk:
In florid things but small its share.
You'll find it in Rome's squalid Ghetto,
In Algiers at the lazaretto,
In many a grimy slimy lair."

"Well put!" cried Brouwer with ruddled[87] face,
His wine-stained vesture—hardly new—
Buttoned with silver florins true;   270
"*Grime* mark and *slime!*—Squirm not, *Sweet Charles.*"
Slyly, in tone mellifluous
Addressing Carlo Dolce thus,
Fidgety in shy fellowship,
Fastidious even to finger-tip,
And dainty prim: "In Art the sty
Is quite inodorous. Here am I:
I don't paint *smells,* no no, no no,
No more than Huysum here, whose touch
In pinks and tulips takes us so;   280
But haunts that reek may harbor much;
Hey, Teniers? Give us boors at inns,
Mud floor—dark settles—jugs—old bins,
Under rafters foul with fume that blinks
From logs too soggy much to blaze
Which yet diffuse an umberish haze
That beautifies the grime, methinks."
To Rembrandt then: "Your sooty stroke!
'Tis you, old sweep, believe in smoke."
But he, reserved in self-control,   290
Jostled by that convivial droll,
Seemed not to hear, nor silence broke.

V

One of the greater Dutchmen dirges the departed
three-deckers of De Ruyter and Van Tromp. To divert

from which monody, a Lesser Master verbally hits off
a kitchen-dresser, and in such sort as to evoke commen-
dation from one [of] the Grand Masters, who never-
theless proposes a certain transmuting enhancement in
the spirit of the latter's own florid and allegoric style.

Here Van der Velde, who dreamy heard
Familiar Brouwer's unanswered word,
Started from thoughts leagues off at sea:
"Believe in smoke? Why, ay, such smoke
As the swart old *Dunderberg* erst did fold—
When, like the cloud-voice from the mountain rolled,
Van Tromp through the bolts of her broadside spoke—
Bolts heard by me!" And lapsed in thought   *300*
Of yet other frays himself had seen
When, fired by adventurous love of Art,
With De Ruyter he'd cruised, yea, a tar had been.
Reminiscent he sat. Some lion-heart old,
Austerely aside, on latter days cast,
So muses on glories engulfed in the Past,
And laurelled ones stranded or overrolled
By eventful Time.—He awoke anon,
Or, rather, his dream took audible tone.—
Then filling his cup:
                              "On Zealand's strand   *310*
I saw morn's rays slant 'twixt the bones
Of the oaken *Dunderberg* broken up;
Saw her ribbed shadow on the sand.
Ay—picturesque! But naught atones
For heroic navies, Pan's own ribs and knees,
But a story now that storied made the seas!"
There the gray master-hand marine
Fell back with desolated mien
Leaving the rest in fluttered[88] mood
Disturbed by such an interlude   *320*
Scarce genial in over earnest tone,

Nor quite harmonious with their own.
To meet and turn the tide-wave there,
"For me, friends," Gerard Douw here said,
Twirling a glass with sprightly air,
"I too revere forefather Eld,
Just feeling's mine too for old oak,
One here am I with Van der Velde;
But take thereto in grade that's lesser:
I like old oak in kitchen-dresser,   330
The same set out with delf ware olden
And well-scoured copper sauce-pans—golden
In aureate rays that on the hearth
Flit like fairies or frisk in mirth.
Oak buffet too; and, flung thereon,
As just from evening-market won,
Pigeons and prawns, bunched carrots bright,
Gilled fish, clean radish red and white,
And greens and cauliflowers, and things
The good wife's good provider brings;   340
All these too touched with fire-side light.
On settle there, a Phillis pleasant
Plucking a delicate fat pheasant.
Agree, the picture's *picturesque*."

"Ay, hollow beats all Arabesque!
But Phillis? Make her Venus, man,
Peachy and plump; and for the pheasant,
No fowl but will prove acquiescent
Promoted into Venus' swan;
Then in suffused warm rosy weather   350
Sublime them in sun-cloud together."
The Knight, Sir Peter Paul, 'twas he,
Hatted in rich felt, spick and span,
Right comely in equipment free,
With court-air of Lord Chamberlain:
"So! 'twere a canvas meet for donor.

What say you, Paolo of Verona?"—[89]
Appealing here.
                    "Namesake, 'tis good!"
Laughed the frank master, gorgeous fellow,
Whose raiment matched his artist-mood: *360*
Gold chain over russet velvet mellow—
A chain of honor; silver-gilt,
Gleamed at his side a jewelled hilt.
In feather high, in fortune free,
Like to a Golden Pheasant, he.
"By Paul, 'tis good, Sir Peter! Yet
Our Hollander here his picture set
In flushful light much like your own,
Tho' but from kitchen-ingle thrown.—
But come to Venice, Gerard,—do,"   *370*
Round turning genial on him there,
"Her sunsets,—there's hearth-light for you;
And matter for you on the Square.
To Venice, Gerard!"
                    "O, we Dutch,
Signor, know Venice, like her much.
Our unction thence we got, some say,
Tho' scarce our subjects, nor your touch."—
"To Saint Mark's again, Mynheer, and stay!
We're Cyprus wine.—But, Monsieur," turning
To Watteau nigh: "You vow in France,   *380*
This *Pittoresque* our friends advance,
How seems it to your ripe discerning?
If by a sketch it best were shown,
A hand I'll try, yes, venture one:—
A chamber on the Grand Canal
In season, say, of Carnival.
A revel reigns; and, look, the host
Handsome as Cæsar Borgia sits—"

"Then Borgia be it, bless your wits!"

Snapped Spagnoletto, late engrossed   390
In splenetic mood, now riling up;
I'll lend you hints.⁹⁰ And let His Grace
Be launching, ay, the loving-cup
Among the princes in the hall
At Sinigaglia: You recall?
I mean those gudgeons whom his smile
Flattered to sup, ere yet awhile,
In Hades with Domitian's lords.
Let sunny frankness charm his air,
His raiment lace with silver cords,   400
Trick forth the *'Christian statesman'* there.
And, mind ye, don't forget the pall;
Suggest it—how politeness ended:
Let lurk in shade of rearward wall
Three bravoes by the arras splendid."

VI

The superb gentleman from Verona, pleasantly parry-
ing the not-so-pleasant little man from Spain, resumes
his off-hand sketch.—Toward Jan Steen, sapient spend-
thrift in shabby raiment, smoking his tavern-pipe and
whiffing out his unconventional philosophy, Watteau,
habited like one of his own holiday-courtiers in the Park
of Fontainebleau, proves himself, tho' but in a minor
incident, not lacking in considerate courtesy humane.

"O, O, too picturesque by half!"
Was Veronese's turning laugh;
"Nay, nay: but see, on ample round
Of marble table silver-bound
Prince Comus, in mosaic, crowned;   410
Vin d'oro there in crystal flutes—
Shapely as those, good host of mine,
You summoned ere our *Sillery* fine

We popped to Bacchus in salutes;—
Well, cavaliers in manhood's flower
Fanning the flight o' the fleeing hour;
Dames, too, like sportful dolphins free:—
Silks iridescent, wit and glee.
Midmost, a Maltese knight of honor
Toasting and clasping his Bella Donna;   *420*
One arm round waist with pressure soft,
Returned in throbbed transporting rhyme;
A hand with minaret-glass aloft,
Pinnacle of the jovial prime!
What think? I daub, but daub it, true;[91]
And yet some dashes there may do."

The Frank assented. But Jan Steen,
With fellowly yet thoughtful mien,
Puffing at skull-bowl pipe serene,
"Come, a brave sketch, no mincing one!   *430*
And yet, adzooks, to this I hold,
Be it cloth of frieze or cloth of gold,
All's picturesque beneath the sun;
I mean, all's picture; death and life
Pictures and pendants, nor at strife—
No, never to hearts that muse thereon.
For me, 'tis life, plain life, I limn—
Not satin-glossed and flossy-fine
(Our Turburg's forte here, good for him).
No, but the life that's *wine and brine,*   *440*
The mingled brew; the thing as spanned
By Jan who kept the Leyden tavern
And every rollicker fellowly scanned—
And, under his vineyard, lo, a cavern!
But jolly is Jan, and never in picture
Sins against sinners by Pharisee stricture.
Jan o' the Inn, 'tis he, for ruth,

Dashes with fun art's canvas of truth."

Here Veronese swerved him round
With glance well-bred of ruled surprise 450
To mark a prodigal so profound,
Nor too good-natured to be wise.

Watteau, first complimenting Steen,
Ignoring there his thriftless guise,
Took up the fallen thread between.
Tho' unto Veronese bowing—
Much pleasure at his sketch avowing;
Yet fain he would in brief convey
Some added words—perchance, in way
To vindicate his own renown, 460
Modest and true in pictures done:
"Ay, Signor; but—your leave—admit,
Besides such scenes as well you've hit,
Your *Pittoresco* too abounds
In life of old patrician grounds
For centuries kept for luxury mere:
Ladies and lords in mimic dress
Playing at shepherd and shepherdess
By founts that sing *The sweet o' the year!*
But, Signor—how! what's this? you seem 470
Drugged off in miserable dream.
How? What impends?"
                              "Barbaric doom!
Worse than the Constable's sack of Rome!"
"Ceil, ceil! The matter? tell us, do."

"This cabbage *Utility, parbleu!*
What shall insure the Carnival—
The gondola—the Grand Canal?
That palaced duct they'll yet deplete,
Improve it to a huckster's street.

And why? Forsooth, *malarial!*"[92]   *480*
There ending with an odd grimace,
Reflected from the Frenchman's face.

VII

Brouwer inurbanely applauds Veronese, and is con-
vivially disrespectful in covert remark on M. Angelo
across the table.—Raphael's concern for the melancholy
estate of Albert Durer. And so forth.

At such a sally, half grotesque,
That indirectly seemed to favor
His *own* view of the Picturesque,
Suggesting Dutch canals in savor;
Pleased Brouwer gave a porpoise-snort,
A trunk-hose Triton trumping glee.
Claude was but moved to smile in thought;
The while Velasquez, seldom free,   *490*
Kept council with himself sedate,
Isled in his ruffed Castilian state,
Viewing as from aloft the mien
Of Hals hilarious, Lippi, Steen,
In chorus frolicking back the mirth
Of Brouwer, careless child of earth;
Salvator Rosa posing nigh
With sombre-proud satiric eye.

But Poussin, he, with antique air,
Complexioned like a marble old,   *500*
Unconscious kept in merit there
Art's pure Acropolis in hold.[93]

For Durer, piteous good fellow—
(His Agnes seldom let him mellow)
His Sampson locks, dense, curling brown,

Sideways umbrageously fell down,
Enshrining so the Calvary face.
Hals says, Angelico sighed to Durer,
Taking to heart his desperate case,
"Would, friend, that Paradise might allure her!"   *510*
If Fra Angelico so could wish
(That fleece that fed on lilies fine)
Ah, saints! the head in Durer's dish,
And how may hen-pecked seraph pine!

For Leonardo, lost in dream,
His eye absorbed the effect of light
Rayed thro' red wine in glass—a gleam
Pink on the polished table bright;
The subtle brain, convolved in snare,
Inferring and over-refining there.   *520*

But Michael Angelo, brief his stay,
And, even while present, sat withdrawn.
Irreverent Brouwer in sly way
To Lippi whispered, "Brother good,
How to be free and hob-nob with
Yon broken-nosed old monolith
Kin to the battered colossi-brood?
Challenged by rays of sunny wine
Not Memnon's stone in olden years
Ere magic fled, had grudged a sign!   *530*
Water he drinks, he munches bread.
And on pale lymph of fame may dine.
Cheaply is this Archangel fed!"

VIII

Herein, after noting certain topics glanced at by the
company, the Marquis concludes the entertainment by
rallying the Old Guard of Greybeards upon the somno-

lent tendency of their years. This, with polite consider-
ateness, he does under the fellowly form of the plural
pronoun. Finally he recommends them to give audience,
by way of pastime, to the "Afternoon in Naples" of his
friend and disciple Jack Gentian. And so the genial
Frenchman takes French leave, a judicious way[94] of part-
ing as best sparing the feelings on both sides.

So Brouwer, the droll. But others sit
Flinting at whiles scintillant wit
On themes whose tinder takes the spark,
Igniting some less light perchance—
The *romanesque* in men of mark;
And this, Shall coming time enhance
Through favoring influence, or abate   *540*
Character picturesquely great—
That rumored age whose scouts advance?
And costume too they touch upon:
The Cid, his net-work shirt of mail,
And Garibaldi's woolen one:
In higher art would each avail
So just expression nobly grace—
Declare the hero in the face?

On themes that under orchards old
The chapleted Greek would frank unfold,   *550*
And Socrates, a spirit divine,
Not alien held to cheerful wine,
That reassurer of the soul—
On these they chat.

                    But more whom they,[95]
Even at the Inn of Inns do meet—
The Inn with greens above the door:
There the mahogany's waxed how bright,
And, under chins such napkins white.

Never comes the mart's intrusive roar,
Nor heard the shriek that starts the train, 560
Nor teasing telegraph clicks again,
No news is cried, and hurry is no more—
For us, whose lagging cobs delay
To win that tavern free from cumber,
Old lads, in saddle shall we slumber?

Here's Jack, whose genial sigh-and-laugh
Where youth and years[96] yblend in sway,
Is like the alewife's half-and-half;
Jack Gentian, in whose beard of gray 570
Persistent threads of auburn tarry
Like streaks of amber after day
Down in the west; you'll not miscarry
Attending here his bright-and-sombre
Companion good to while the way
With Naples in the Times of Bomba.

END[97]

A SEQUEL

Touching the Grand Canal's depletion
If Veronese did but feign,
Grave frolic of a gay Venetian
Masking in Jeremy his vein; 580
Believe, that others too may gambol
In syllables as light—yea, ramble
All over each aesthetic park,
Playing, as on the violin,
One random theme our dames to win—
The picturesque in Men of Mark.
Nor here some lateral points they shun,
And pirouette on this, for one:
That rumored Age, whose scouts advance,

Musters it one chivalric lance?
Or shall it foster or abate
Qualities picturesquely great?   *590*

There's Garibaldi, off-hand hero,
A very Cid Campeadór,
Lion-Nemesis of Naples' Nero—
But, tut, why tell that story o'er!
A natural knight-errant, truly,
Nor priding him in parrying fence,
But charging at the helm-piece—hence
By statesmen deemed a lord unruly.
Well now, in days the gods decree,   *600*
Toward which the levellers scything move
(The Sibyl's page consult, and see)
Could this our Cid a hero prove?
What meet emprise? What plumed career?
No challenges from crimes flagitious
When all is uniform in cheer;
For Tarquins—none would be extant,
Or, if they were, would hardly daunt,
Ferruling brats, like Dionysius;
And Mulciber's sultans, overawed,   *610*
In dumps and mumps, how far from menace,
Tippling some claret about deal board
Like Voltaire's kings at inn in Venice.
In fine, the dragons penned or slain,
What for St. George would then remain!

A don[98] of rich erratic tone,
By jaunty junior club-men known
As one who, buckram in demur,
Applies then the Johnsonian *Sir;*
'Twas he that rollicked thus of late   *620*
Filliped by turn of chance debate.
Repeat he did, or vary more

The same conceit, in devious way
Of grandees with dyed whiskers hoar
Tho' virile yet: "Assume, and say
The Red Shirt Champion's natal day
Is yet to fall in promised time,
Millennium of the busy bee;
How would he fare in such a Prime?
By Jove, sir, not so bravely, see!   *630*
Never he'd quit his trading trips,
Perchance, would fag in trade at desk,
Or, slopped in slimy slippery sludge,
Lifelong on Staten Island drudge,
Melting his tallow, Sir, dipping his *dips,*
Scarce savoring much of the Picturesque!"
"Pardon," here purled a cultured wight
Lucid with transcendental light;
"Pardon, but tallow none nor trade
When, thro' this Iron Age's reign   *640*
The Golden one comes in again;
That's on the card."
                          "She plays the spade!
Delving days, Sir, heave in sight—
Digging days, Sir; and, sweet youth,
They'll set on edge the sugary tooth:
A treadmill—Paradise they plight."

Let be, and curb this rhyming race!—

      Angel o' the Age! advance, God speed.
      Harvest us all good grain in seed;
      But sprinkle, do, some drops of grace   *650*
      Nor polish us into commonplace.

NAPLES IN THE TIME OF BOMBA
as told by
MAJOR JACK GENTIAN

Chartering a nondescript holiday hack at his Neapolitan inn, the tourist Jack Gentian drives out, and is unexpectedly made the object of a spontaneous demonstration more to be prized by an appreciative recipient than the freedom of the city of New Jerusalem presented in a diamond box by a deputation from the Crown Council of Seraphim.

Behind a span whose cheery pace
Accorded well with gala trim—
Each harness,[99] in arch triumphal reared,
With festive ribbons fluttering gay;
In Bomba's Naples sallying forth[100]
In season when the vineyards mellow,
Suddenly turning a corner round—
Ha, happy to meet you, Punchinello!

And, merrily there, in license free,
The crowd they caper, droll as he;   *10*
While, arch as any, rolled in fun,
Such tatterdemalions, many a one!

We jounced along till, just ahead,
Nor far from shrine in niche of wall,
A stoppage fell. His[101] rug or bed
In midmost way a tumbler spread,
A posturing mountebank withal;
Who, though his stage was out of doors,
Brought down the house in jolly applause.

"Signor," exclaims my charioteer,   *20*
Turning, and reining up, the while

Trying to touch his jaunty hat;
But here, essaying to condense
Such opposite movements into one
Failing, and letting fall his whip,
"His Excellency stops the way!"
His Excellency there, meanwhile—
Reversed in stature, legs aloft,
And hobbling jigs on hands for heels—
Gazed up with blood-shot brow that told   *30*
The tension of that nimble play—
Gazed up as martyred Peter might;
And, noting me in landeau-seat
(*Milor,* there he opined, no doubt)
Brisk somersetted back, and stood
Urbanely bowing, then gave place;
While, tickled at my puzzled plight,
Yet mindful that a move was due,
And knowing me a stranger there,
With one consent the people part   *40*
Yielding a passage, and with eyes
Of friendly fun,—how courteous too!
Catching an impulse from their air,
To feet I spring, my beaver doff
And broadcast wave a blithe salute.
In genial way how humorsome,
What pleased responses of surprise;
From o'er the Alps, and so polite!
They clap their hands in frank acclaim,
Matrons in door-ways nod and smile,   *50*
From balcony roguish girls laugh out
Or kiss their fingers, rain their nosegays down.
At such a shower—laugh, clap, and flower—
My horses shy, the landeau tilts,
Distractedly the driver pulls.

But I, Jack Gentian, what reck I,

The popular hero, object sole
Of this ovation!—I aver
No viceroy, king, nor emperor,
Panjandrum Grand, conquistador—   *60*
Not Caesar's self in car aloft
Triumphal on the Sacred Way,
No, nor young Bacchus through glad Asia borne,
Pelted with grapes, exulted so
As I in hackney-landeau here
Jolting and jouncing thro' the waves
Of confluent commoners who in glee
Good natured past before my prow.

II

    Arrested by a second surprise not in harmony with the
first, he is thereupon precipitated into meditations more
or less profound, though a little mixed, as they say.

Flattered along by following cheers
We sped; I musing here in mind,   *70*
Beshrew me, needs be overdrawn
Those shocking stories bruited wide,
In England which I left but late,
Touching dire tyranny in Naples.
True[102] freedom is to be care-free!
And care-free seem the people here
A truce indeed they seem to keep,
Gay truce to care and all her brood.

But, look: what mean yon surly walls?
A fortress? and in heart of town?   *80*
Even so. And rapt I stare thereon.
The battlements black-beetling hang
Over the embrasures' tiers of throats
Whose enfilading tongues seem trained

Less to beat alien foemen off
Than awe the town. "Rabble!" they said,
Or in dumb threatening seemed to say,
"Revolt, and we will rake your lanes!"

But what strange quietude of wall!   *90*
While musing if response would be
Did tourist on the clampt gate tap
Politely there with slender cane—
Abrupt, to din condensed of drums
And blast of thronged trumps trooping first,
Right and left with clangor and clash
The double portals outward burst
Before streamed thronged[103] bayonets that flash
Like lightning's sortie from the cloud.
Storming from the gloomy tower
Tempestuous thro' the carverned arch,   *100*
Like one long lance they lunge along,
A thousand strong of infantry!
The captains like to torches flaring,
Red plumes and scarlet sashes blown,
Bare sword in hand audacious gleaming;
While, like ejected lava rolled,
The files on files are vomited forth
Eruptive from their crater belched!
Sidelong, in vulpine craven sort,
On either flank at louring brows   *110*
Of tag-rag who before their sortie
Divide in way how all unlike
Their parting late before my wheels!
Who makes this sortie? who? and why?
Anon I learned. Sicilians, these—
Sicilians from Palermo shipped
In meet exchange for hirelings lent
From Naples here to hold the Isle;
And daily thus in seething town

From fort to fort are trooping, streamed   *120*
To threaten, intimidate, and cow.

Flaunting the overlording flag,
Thumping the domineering drum,
With insolent march of blustering arms
They clean put out the festive stir,
Ay, quench the popular fun.
The fun they quench, but scarce the hate
In bridled imprecations pale
Of brooding hearts vindictive there,
The deadlier bent for rasping curb,   *130*
Through mutterings like deep thunder low,
Couched thunder ere the leaping bolt,
The swaggering troops and bullying trumpets go.

They fleet—they fade. And, altered much,
In serious sort my way I hold,
Till revery, taking candor's tone,
With optimistic influence plead:
Sad, bad, confess; but solace bides!
For much has Nature done, methinks,
In offset here with kindlier aim.   *140*
If bayonets flash, what vineyards glow!
Of all these hells of wrath and wrong
How little feels the losel light
Who, thrown upon the odorous sod
In this indulgent clime of charm
Scarce knows a thought or feels a care
Except to take his careless pleasure:
A fig for Bomba! life is fair
Squandered in superabundant leisure!

Ay, but ye ragamuffs cutting pranks   *150*
About the capering mountebanks

Was *that* indeed mirth's true elation?
Or even in some a patched despair,
Bravery in tatters debonair,
True devil-may-care dilapidation?
Well, be these rubs even how they may,
Smart cock-plumes in yon headstalls dance,
Each harness[104] with ribbons flutters gay,
I see at pole our wreath advance: *160*
Inodorous muslin garland—true:
Impostor, but of jocund hue!
Ah, could one but realities rout,
A holiday-world it were, no doubt.
But Naples, sure she lacks not cheer,
Religion, it is jubilee here—
Feast follows festa thro' the year;
And then such Nature all about!
No surly moor of forge and mill,
She charms us glum barbarians still,
Fleeing from frost, bad bread, or duns,   *170*
Despotic *Biz,* and devils blue,
And there's our pallid invalid ones,
Their hollow eyes the scene survey;
They win this clime of more than spice,
These myrtled shores, to wait the boat
That ferries (so the pilots say),
Yes, ferries to the isles afloat,
The floating Isles of Paradise
In God's Ægean far away!
O, scarce in trivial tenor all,   *180*
Much less to mock man's mortal sigh,
Those syllables proverbial fall,
Naples, see Naples, and—then die!

But hark: yon low note rising clear;
A singer!—rein up, charioteer!

III

Opening with a fervent little lyric which, if obscure in
purport or anyway questionable to a Hyperborean pro-
fessor of Agnostic Moral Philosophy, will nevertheless
to readers as intelligently sympathetic as our honest nar-
rator, be transparent enough and innocent as the Thirty
Thousand Virgins of Cologne.

"Name me, do, that dulcet Donna
    Whose perennial gifts engaging
Win the world to dote upon her
    In meridian never ageing!

Look, in climes beyond the palms   *190*
Younger sisters bare young charms—
    She the mellower graces!
Ripened heart maturely kind,
St. Martin's summer of the mind,
And pathos of the years behind—
    More than empty faces!"

Who sings? Behold him under bush
Of vintner's ivy nigh a porch,
His rag-fair raiment botched and darned
But face much like a Delphic coin's   *200*
New disinterred with clinging soil.
Tarnished Apollo!—But let pass.
Best here be heedful, yes, and chary,
Sentiment nowadays waxeth wary,
And idle the ever-cooked *Alas*.

IV

Quick as lightning he is presented with a festive flower

by the titillating fingers of a flying Peri, who thereupon
spinning in pirouette, evaporates or vanishes.

Advancing now, we passed hard by
A regal court where under drill
Drawn up in line the palace-guard
Behind tall iron pickets spiked
With gilded barbs, in martial din   *210*
Clanged down their muskets on the pave.
Some urchins small looked on, and men
With eye-lids squeezed, yet letting out
A flame as of quick lightning thin;
The Captain of the guard meanwhile,
A nervous corpulence, on these
Stealing a restive sidelong glance.
A curve. And rounding by the bay
Nigh[105] Edens parked along the verge,
Brief halt was made amid the press;   *220*
And, instantaneous thereupon,
A buoyant nymph on odorous wing
Alighting on the landeau-step,
Half hovering like a humming-bird,
A flower pinned to my lapelle,
Letting a thrill from finger brush
(Sure, unaware) the sensitive chin;
Yes, badged me in a twinkling bright
With O a red and royal rose;
A rose just flowering from the bud   *230*
Received my tribute, random coins,
Beaming received it, chirped adieu,
Twirled on her pivot and—was gone!
An opening came; and in a trice
The horses went, my landeau rocked,
The ribbons streamed; while, ruddy now,
Flushed with the rose's reflex bloom,

I dwelt no more on things amiss:
Come, take thine ease; lean back, my soul;
The world let spin; what signifies?   *240*
Look, she, the flower-girl—what recks she
Of Bomba's sortie? what indeed!
Fine sortie of her own, the witch,
But now she made upon my purse,
And even a craftier sally too!

V

Giving way to thoughts less cheerful than archaic, he
is checked by a sportive sally from the Rose. But is
anew troubled, catching sight of an object attesting a
Power even more nitrous and menacing than the Bomb-
King himself. In short, another and greater crowned
artilleryman, a capricious dominator, impossible to de-
throne, and reigning by right incontestably divine. Pon-
dering which discouraging fact, once more our genial
friend is twitted by the festive Mentor.

"Signor, turn here?" And turn we did,
Repassing scenes that charmed erewhile,
Nor less could charm reviewed even now.
What blandishment in clime, or else
What subtler influence, my rose,[106]   *250*
From thee exhaled, thou Lydian one,
Seductive here could flatter me
Even in emotion not unfelt
While fleeting from that warmish pair!
If, taking tone indeed from them,
No lightsome thought awhile prevailed,
Devious it drifted[107] like a dream.
I mused on Virgil, here inurned
On Pausilippo, legend tells—
Here on the slope that pledges ease to pain,   *260*

For him a pledge assuredly true
If here indeed his ashes be—
Rome's laureate in Rome's palmy time;
Nor less whose epic's undertone
In volumed numbers rolling bland,
Chafing against the metric bound,
Plains like the South Sea ground-swell heaved
Against the palm-isle's halcyon strand.

What Mohawk of a mountain lours!   *270*
A scalp-lock of Tartarian smoke
Thin streaming forth from tawny brow,
One heel on painted Pompeii set,
And one on Hercules 'whelmed town!

The Siren's seat for pleasurists lies
Betwixt two threatening bombardiers,
Their mortars loaded, linstocks lit—
Vesuvius yonder—Bomba here.
Events may Bomba's batteries spike:
But how with thee, sulphurious Hill
Whose vent far hellward reaches down!   *280*

Ah, funeral urns of time antique
Inwrought with flowers in gala play,[108]
Whose form and bacchanal dance in freak,[109]
Even as of pagan time ye speak
Type ye what Naples is alway?
Yes, round these curved volcanic shores,
Vined urn of ashes, bed on bed,
Abandonment as thoughtless pours[110]
As when the revelling pagan led.
And here again I droopt the brow,   *290*
And, lo, again I saw the Rose,
The red red ruddy and royal Rose!
Expanded more from bud but late,

Sensuous it lured, and took the tone
Of some light taunting Cyprian gay
In shadow deep of college-wall
Startling some museful youth afoot—
"Mooning in mind? Ah, lack-a-day!"[111]

VI

Uninfluenced by the pranks and rhymes of certain
Merry Andrews of the beach, he unaccountably falls
into an untimely fit of historic reminiscences. For which
dereliction, the Rose, now in a pleading mood, touchingly
upbraids him. But again he relapses, notwithstanding an
animated call, subsequently heard, to regale himself with
ruddy apples and sweet oranges.

I turned me short; and, timely now,
Beheld this scene: damsels sun-burnt,   *300*
In holiday garb with tinsel trimmed;
And men and lads behind them ranged
About a carpet on the beach,
Whereon a juggler in brocade
Made rainbows of his glittering balls,
Cascading them with dexterous sleight;
And as from hand to hand they flew
With minglings[112] of interior din,
He trilled a ditty deftly timed
To every lilted motion light:—   *310*

    "The balls, hey! the balls,
    Cascatella of balls—
    Baseless arches I toss up in air!
    Spinning we go,—
    Now over, now under;
    High Jack is Jack low,
    And never a blunder!
    Come hither—go thither:

But wherefore nowhither?
I lose them—I win them,   *320*
From hand to hand spin them,
Reject them, and seize them,
And toss them, and tease them,
And keep them forever in air,
All to serve but a freak[113] of my glee!

Sport ye thus with your spoonies, ye fair,
For your mirth? nor even forbear
To juggle with Nestors your thralls?
Do ye keep them in play with your smiling and
    frowning,
Your flirting, your fooling, abasing[114] and
    crowning,   *330*
And dance them as I do these balls?"

With that, and hurrying his two hands,
Arching he made his meteors play;
When, lo, like Mercury dropped from heaven,
Precipitate there a tumbler flew,
Alighting on winged feet;[115] then sang,
Dancing at whiles, and beating time,
Clicking his nimble heels together
In hornpipe of the gamesome kid:

    "Over mines, by vines   *340*
    That take hot flavor
    From Vesuvius—
    Hark, in vintage
    Sounds the tabor!

    "In brimstone-colored
    Tights or breeches
    There the Wag-fiend
    Dancing teaches;

"High in wine-press
Hoop elastic   *350*
Pigeon-wings cut
In rite fantastic;
While the black grape,
Spirting, gushing,
Into red wine
Foameth rushing!

"Which wine drinking,
Drowning thinking,
Every night-fall,
Heard in Strada,   *360*
Kiss the doves
And coos the adder!"

While yet I listened, vivid came
A flash of thought that carried me
Back to five hundred years ago.
I saw the panoramic bay
In afternoon beneath me spread—
All Naples from siesta risen
Peopling the benches, barges, moles.
Cooled over blue waves tinkling bland[116]   *370*
Came waftures from Sorrento's vines,
And Queen Joanna, queen and bride,
Sat in her casement by the sea,
Twining three strands of silk and gold
Into a cord how softly strung.
"For what this dainty rope, sweet wife?"
It was the bridegroom who had stolen
Behind her chair, and now first spoke.
"To hang you with, Andrea," she said
Smiling. He shrugged his shoulders; "Nay,   *380*
What need? I'll hang but on your neck."
And straight caressed her; and the bride

Sat mutely passive, smiling still.
For jest he took it.[117] But that night
A rope of twisted silk and gold
Droopt from a balcony[118] where vines
In flower showed violently torn;
And, starlit, thence what tassel swung!
For offset to Eve's serpent twined
In that same sleek and shimmering cord,   390
Quite other scene recurred. In hall
Of Naples here, withal I stood[119]
Before the pale mute-speaking stone
Of seated Agrippina—she
The truest woman that ever wed[120]
In tragic widowhood transfixed;
In cruel craft exiled from Rome
To gaze on Naples' sunny bay,
More sharp to feel her sunless doom.
O ageing face, O youthful form,   400
O listless hand in idle lap,
And, ah, what thoughts of God and man!

But intervening here, my Flower,
Opening yet more in bloom the less,
Maturing toward the wane,—low-breathed,
Again? and quite forgotten me?
You wear an Order,[121] me, the Rose,
To whom the favoring fates allot
A term that shall not bloom outlast;
No future's mine, nor mine a past.   410
Yet I'm the Rose, the flower of flowers.
Ah, let Time's present time suffice,
No Past pertains to Paradise.

Time present. Well, in present time
It chanced a lilting note I heard,
A fruit-girl's, and she fluted this:[122]

"Love-apples, love-apples!
All dew, honey-dew,
From orchards of Cyprus—
Blood-oranges too!   *420*

"Will you buy? prithee, try!
They grew facing south;
See, mutely they languish
To melt in your mouth!

" 'Tis now, take them now
In the hey-day of flush,
While the crisis is on,
And the juices can gush!

"Love-apples, love-apples,
All dew, honey-dew,   *430*
From orchards of Cyprus—
Blood-oranges, too!"

Warbling and proffering them she went,
And passed, and left me as erewhile,
For the dun[123] annals would not down.
Murky along the sunny strand
New spectres streamed from shades below,
Spectres of Naples under Spain,
Phantoms of that incensed Revolt
With whose return Wrath threatens still   *440*
Bomba engirt with guards.—Lo,[124] there,
A throng confused, in arms they pass,
Arms snatched from smithy, forge and shop:
Craftsmen[125] and sailors, peasants, boys,
And swarthier faces dusked between—
Brigands and outlaws; linked with these
Salvator Rosa, and the fierce
Falcone with his fiery school;

Pell-mell with riff-raff, banded all
In league as violent as the sway   *450*
Of feudal claims and foreign lords
Whose iron heel evoked the spark
That fired the populace into flame.
And, see, dark eyes and sunny locks
Of Masaniello, bridegroom young,
Tanned marigold-cheek and tasselled cap;
The darling of the mob; nine days
Their great Apollo; then, in pomp
Of Pandemonium's red parade,
His curled head Gorgoned on the pike,   *460*
And jerked aloft for God to see.
A portent. Yes, and typed the years
Red after-years, and whirl of error
When Freedom linkt with Furies raved
In Carmagnole and cannibal hymn,
Mad song and dance before the ark
From France imported with *The Terror!*
To match the poison, mock the clime,
Hell's cornucopia crammed with crime!
Scarce cheerful here the revery ran.   *470*
Nor did my Rose now intervene,
Full opening out in dust and sun
Which hurried along that given term,
She said would never bloom outlast.

VII

He encounters a prepossessing little tatterdemalion
Triton, shell in hand, dewy in luminous spray of a rain-
bowed fountain. With the precocity of his precocious
tribe, the juvenile Levantine, knowing that there is noth-
ing the populace everywhere more like to hear than
something touching upon themselves, their town and
their period, entertains his street-audience accordingly

with certain improvisations partaking alike of the senti-
ment and devil-may-care incident to the Neapolitan.

By marbles where a fountain rose
In jubilant waters scurrying high
To break in sleet against the blue,
I saw a thing as freshly bright—
A boy, who holding up a shell,
Enamelled part, with pinkish valve   *480*
New dipped in rainbows of the spray,
By mute appeal, with deference touched,
As if invoking Naples' monarch,
Not her mob, attention craved.

A weed of life, a sea-weed he
From the Levant adventuring out;
A cruiser light, like all his clan
Who, in repletion's lust for more,
And penury's strife for daily bread,
As licensed by compassionate heaven   *490*
To privateer it on their wits,
The Mid Sea rove from quay to quay,
At home with Turban, Fez, or Hat;
Ready in French, Italian, Greek—
Linguists at large; alert to serve
As chance interpreters or guides;
Suave in address, with winning ways—
Arch imps of Pandarus, a few;
Others with improvising gift
Of voweled rhyme in antic sort,   *500*
Or passionate, spirited by their sun
That ripens them in early teens;
And some with small brown fingers slim
Busier than the jackdaw's bill.

But *he,* what gravity is his!

Precociously sedate indeed
In beauty sensuously serene.
White-draped, and ranked aloft in choir
A treble clear in rolling laud
Meet would he look on Easter morn.   *510*

The muster round him closing more,
How circumspect he plays his part;
His glance intelligent taking in
The motley miscellaneous groups:
Large-chested porters, swarthy dames
In dress provincial that beseems;
Fishermen bronzed, and barbers curled;
Fat monk with paunched[126] umbrella blue;
The quack, magnific in brocade
Chapeau and aigulets; the wight   *520*
That cobbles shoes in public way;
Mariners in red Phrygian caps.
But, twinkling brief, his liquid glance
Skims one poor figure limp that leans
Listlessly deaf amid the hum.
A purblind man, too, sly he views
With staff before him, pattering thin;
Informers these, perchance, and spies?
So queries one, a craftsman there,
Nudging his fellow, winking back.   *530*
And, verily, rumor long has run
That Bomba's blind men well can see,
His deaf men hear, his dumb men talk.
But never amid the varied throng
The boy a stragging soldier notes
In livery lace declaring him.
Howbeit, some sombre garbs he views:
A Jesuit grave, genteely sleek
In dapper small-clothes and fine hose
Of sable silk, and shovel-hat,   *540*

Hard[127] by a doctor of the law,
In sables, too, with parchment cheek;
A useful man to lawless power,
Expert to legalise the wrong.
The twain, brief tarrying there behind,
Went sauntering off ere came the close.

But now the lad, in posture grave,
With sidelong leaning head intent,
The shell's lips to his listening ear,
In modulating tone began: *550*

"Metheglin befuddles this freak o' the sea,
Humming, low humming—in brain a bee!   .

"Hymns it of Naples her myriads warming?
Involute hive in fever of swarming.

"What Hades of sighs in irruption suppressed,
Suffused with huzzahs that buzz in arrest!

"Neapolitans, ay, 'tis the soul of the shell
Intoning your Naples, Parthenope's bell.

"O, couch of the Siren renowned thro' the sea
That enervates Salerno, seduces Baiæ;   *560*

"I attend you, I hear;[128] but how to resolve
The complex of conflux your murmurs involve!"

He paused, as after prelude won;
Abrupt then in recitative, he:[129]

    "Hark, the stir[130]
    The ear invading:

"Crowds on crowds
All promenading;

"Clatter and clink   570
Of cavalcading;

"*Yo-heave-ho!*
From ships unlading;

"Funeral dole,
Thro' arches fading;

"*All hands round!*
In masquerading;

"Litany low—
High rodomontading;

"*Grapes, ripe grapes!*   580
In cheer evading;

"Lazarus' plaint
All vines upbraiding;

"*Crack-crick-crack*
Of fusillading!

"Hurly-burly, late and early,
Gossips prating, quacks orating,
    Daft debating:
Furious wild reiteration
And incensed expostulation!

    "Din condensed,   590
    All hubbub summing:[131]

>Larking, laughing,
>Chattering, chaffing,
>Thrumming, strumming
>Singing, jingling
>All commingling—
>Till the *Drum*,

>Rub-a-dub sounded, doubly pounded,
>Redundant in deep din rebounded,
>Deafening all this hive of noises   600
>Babel-tongued with myriad voices,
>Drubs them *dumb!*

>No more larking,
>No more laughing,
>No more chattering,
>Nay, nor chaffing—
>All is *glum!*

>To blab the reason—
>Were out of season,
>For, look, they *come!*   610

>Rub-a-dub, rub-a-dub,
>Rub-a-double-dub-dub,
>Rub-a-double-dub-dub- o' the drum!"

VIII

In which the young Impudence ventures to treat with sly levity even so sanctioned an abstraction as "the powers that be."[132]

Alert in his young senses five
The lad had caught the wafted roll
Of Bomba's barbarous tom-toms thumped,

And improvised the beat. Anon
The files wheeled into open view.
A second troop a thousand strong
With band and banners, flourished blades,   *620*
Launched from a second cannoned den
And now in countermarch thereon;
The great drum-major towering up
In aigulets and tinsel tags—
Pagoda glittering in Cathay!

Arch whiskerando and gigantic
A grandiose magnifico antic[133]
Tossing his truncheon in the van.
A hifalutin exaggeration,
Barbaric in his bearskin shako,   *630*
Of bullying Bomba's puffed elation
And blood-and-thunder proclamation,
A braggadocio Bourbon-Draco!

While yet the bayonets flashed along
And all was silent save the drum,
Then first it was I chanced to note
Some rose-leaves fluttering off in air,
While on my lap lay wilted ones.
Ah, Rose, that should not bloom outlast
Now leaf by leaf art leaving me?   *640*

But here anew the lad broke in:—

> "Lo, the King's men
> They go marching!
> O, the instep
> Haughty arching!—
> *Live the King!*

"What's the grin for—

Queer grimacing?
Who, yon grenadiers
    Outfacing,   *650*
Here dare sing
    Ironically—
Live the King?"

But there, a comely wine-wife plump,
A bustling motherly good body
Who all along in fidgety sort
Concern had shown, and tried her way
To push up to this imp satiric,
Got next him now, and clapping hand
Across his mouth, she whispered him.   *660*
He heard; then, turning toward the throng,
"She says, Young chick come down a peg,
Nor risk being pent anew in egg."
Castel dell Ovo here was meant,
The oval fortress on the bay,
Hiving its captives in sea-cells;
Nor patriots only, plotters deemed,
But talkers, rhymesters, every kind
Of indiscreetly innocent mind.
Nor less the volatile audience—late   *670*
Grinding their teeth at Bomba's guards,
Were tickled by the allusive pun,
Howbeit, the boy here made an end;
And dulcet now, with decent air,
Of mild petitionary grace:
"Carlo am I, some *carlins* then!"
He twitched his sash up, scarlet rag,
Blithely in bonnet caught the coins,
Then disappeared beyond the marge
To dice with other imps as young,   *680*
Ere yet a little and his star
Evanish like the Pleiad lost.

IX

Herein, if Jack Gentian, ever reputed a man of verac-
ity, is to be credited, so thin a thing as a wafer made of
a little flour and water, and so forth, the same being
viewless, or carefully covered from view, proves of far
more efficacy in bringing a semi-insurgent populace to
their knees than all the bombs, bayonets, and fusillades
of the despot of Naples.

The younker[134] faded, voice and all—
He faded, and his carol died,
Forgot anon in shifted scene;
For, hark, what slender chimes are these
On zephyr borne? And, look, the folk
In one consent of strange accord,
Part, and in expectation stand;
Yet scarce as men who mirth await—   690
More like to crowds that wait[135] eclipse,
So gravely sobering seems to fall
Those light lilt chimes now floating near,
In harbinger of—what behind?
It comes; a corpulent form erect,
And holds what looks a Titan stem
Of lily-of-the-vale, the buds
A congregation of small bells—
Small, silver, and of dulcet tone,
Drooping from willowy light wires;   700
Behind, in square, four boys in albs[136]
Whose staves uphold a canopy,
And, under this, a shining priest
Who to some death-bed bears the *host*
In mystic state before him veiled.

A hush falls; and the people drop
Stilly and instantaneous all

As plumps the apple ripe from twig
And cushions motionless in sod.
My charioteer reins short—transfixed;   *710*
The very mountebanks, they kneel;
And idlers, all along and far,
Bow over as the *host* moves on—
Bow over, and for time remain
Like to Pompeiian masquers caught
With fluttering garb in act of flight,
For ages glued in deadly drift.
But, look, the Rose, brave Rose, is where?
Last petals falling, and its soul
Of musk dissolved in empty air!   *720*

And here this draught at hazard drawn,
Like squares of fresco newly dashed,
Cools, hardens, nor will more receive,
Scarce even the touch that mends a slip:
The plaster sets; quietus—bide.

Let bide; nor all the piece esteem
A medley mad of each extreme;
Since, in those days, gyved Naples, stung
By tickling, tantalising pain,
Like tried St. Anthony giddy hung   *730*
Betwixt the tittering hussies twain:
She sobbed, she laughed, she rattled her chain;
Till the Red Shirt proved signal apt
Of danger ahead to Bomba's son,
And presently freedom's thunder clapt,
And lo, he fell from toppling throne—
Fell down, like Dagon on his face,
And ah, the unfeeling populace!

But Garibaldi—Naples' host
Uncovers to her deliverer's ghost,   *740*

While down time's aisle, mid clarions clear
Pale glory walks by valor's bier.

AFTER-PIECE[137]

Skimming over the Poem a book, he tables it, and
after sipping a cup of peevish tea, dwells upon the first
verse.

Pale "Glory-walks-by-Valor's-bier."
Now why a catafalque in close?
No relish I that stupid cheer
Ringing down the curtain on the Rose.

NOTES

1. *Poetry and the Age* (New York: Vintage Books 1953), p. 112.
2. William B. Stein's *The Poetry of Melville's Late Years* (Albany: State University of New York Press 1970), published after the writing of this essay, contains valuable discussions of "Bridegroom Dick," pp. 25–33, and "Grandvin," pp. 227–69, as well as a fine comment on the prosody of "The Scout Toward Aldie," pp. 6–7.
3. Richard V. Chase, in *Herman Melville* (New York: Macmillan Co. 1949), p. 290, shows a thorough reading of the poem, but offers no critical focus. Richard H. Fogle, in "The Themes of Melville's Later Poetry," *Tulane Studies in English*, XI (1961), 70–72, touches briefly but incisively on some aspects of the poem (Melville's nostalgia, his more mellow attitude toward officers here than in *White–Jacket*, and his sense of the Civil War's complexity).
4. *Collected Poems of Herman Melville* (Chicago: Packard & Co. 1947), p. 470.
5. *The Portable Melville* (New York: Viking Press 1952), p. xx. In *Selected Poems of Herman Melville* (New York: Random House 1970), p. 51, Robert Penn Warren says that in "Bridegroom Dick" "the content of the musing is . . . strictly personal."
6. *A Reader's Guide to Herman Melville* (New York: Farrar, Straus & Cudahy 1962), p. 217.
7. *Herman Melville* (New York: Twayne Publishers 1963), p. 126.
8. *Selected Poems of Herman Melville* (Garden City: Doubleday 1964), p. 182.
9. *The Example of Melville* (Princeton: Princeton University Press 1962), p. 198.
10. "Melville and the Civil War," *Tulane Studies in English*, IX (1959), 82.
11. *Herman Melville* (Berkeley: University of California Press, 1951), p. 322.
12. *Example of Melville*, p. 208.

13. "Melville's Battle-Pieces," *U. of Texas Studies in English,* XXXV (1956), p. 111.
14. *Melville,* pp. 275–77. The story is in fact told with tension and economy.
15. *Melville and the Civil War,* p. 81.
16. *Ibid.*
17. L. S. Mansfield, "Melville's Comic Articles on Zachary Taylor," *American Literature,* IX (1938), 411–18.
18. *Melville,* pp. 276–77.
19. *American Renaissance* (New York: Oxford University Press 1941), p. 494.
20. *Pacifism and Rebellion in the Writings of Herman Melville* (The Hague: Mouton, 1964), p. 49.
21. "Melville the Poet," *Melville: A Collection of Critical Essays,* ed. Richard V. Chase (Englewood Cliffs, New Jersey: Prentice-Hall, 1962), pp. 153–55.
22. This concern is expressed with particular urgency in the prose "Supplement" to *Battle-Pieces.*
23. *Life and Times of Frederick Douglass,* Centenary Edition (New York: Pathway Press 1941), pp. 422–24.
24. Vincent, p. 456.
25. *Herman Melville and the American National Sin,* a Harvard dissertation, 1959, summarized in *Directory of Melville Dissertations,* compiled by Tyrus Hillway and Hershel Parker (Evanston, Northwestern Univ., 1962), p. 44. In his facsimile edition of *Battle-Pieces* (Gainesville, Scholars' Facsimiles & Reprints: 1960), p. xix. Kaplan refers to Melville's "single poem on the Negro as a person," ignoring the "slave" in "Aldie."
26. In this poem Melville imagines the gun facing Charleston as a "coal-black Angel / With a thick Afric lip" who "dwells (like the hunted and harried) / In a swamp . . ." and whose breath "is blastment."
27. Here the poet explains that the enemy had buried his heavy guns along with the dead, hoping to use them later, but that "subsequently the negroes exposed the stratagem."
28. "Misgivings," line 7.
29. *Some Aspects of the Treatment of Negro Characters by Five Representative American Novelists,* a University of Wisconsin dissertation, 1952, summarized in Hillway and Parker, p. 24.
30. *Herman Melville* (New York: Sloane, 1950) p. 280.
31. Howard, pp. 329–30, allows that the poem makes a "passing comment" on the Gilded Age, but he sees it as in the main an expres-

140   MELVILLE'S POETRY

sion of Melville's enthusiasm for painting.

32. *Great Short Works of Herman Melville* (New York: Harper & Row 1970), p. 396.
33. *Pacifism and Rebellion,* p. 183.
34. *Collected Poems,* pp. viii–ix. Fogle, in "The Themes of Melville's Later Poetry," p. 82, also guesses that "Grandvin" was written "between 1857 and 1859."
35. Arvin, p. 209.
36. *Critical Essays,* p. 9.
37. *Melville,* p. 329. *Poetry of Melville's Late Years,* pp. 27–29, 228–31, disputes Howard's view.
38. *Ibid.,* p. 330.
39. It is worth noting that Hoffman's increasingly generous treatment of the foe in his Mexican War poems parallels Melville's position toward the South in the Civil War, and that Hoffman, like Melville, had satirized Gen. Taylor in prose during the Mexican War; see Homer F. Barnes, *Charles Fenno Hoffman* (New York, Columbia University Press 1930), pp. 267–68, and Aaron Kramer, *The Prophetic Tradition in American Poetry, 1835–1900* (Rutherford, N.J.: Fairleigh Dickinson University Press 1968), pp. 55–8, 72.
40. *Selected Poems of Herman Melville* (London: Hogarth Press 1943), p. 6.
41. *Main Currents in American Thought,* vol. 2 (New York, Harcourt, Brace & Co. 1930), p. 259.
42. A further hint of Melville's sensitivity to mob action occurs in the important but generally ignored Civil War poem, "Donelson," when "A shower of broken ice and snow, / In lieu of words, confuted" a Copperhead onlooker outside a news office in New York. Melville remains non-committal, but notes that "each by-stander said–Well suited him." There is a good discussion of "Donelson" in Hennig Cohen's *The Battle-Pieces of Herman Melville* (New York: Thomas Yoseloff 1963), pp. 16–18.
43. For this reason it is doubly distressing that critics involved with Melville's developing attitudes during this period should so completely disregard the poem. Even Bezanson, in his searching introductory essay to *Clarel,* New York: Hendricks House, 1960, fails to avail himself of this source which so valuably illuminates the mood, the imagery, the ideas, and the form of *Clarel.*
44. *Critical Essays,* p. 4.
45. The poems here quoted directly or paraphrased are "The Enthusiast," "The Tuft of Kelp," "Lone Founts," and "Art."
46. Cohen, *Selected Poems,* pp. 248, 256.

47. Vincent, p. 477.
48. Merrell R. Davis and William H. Gilman, eds., *The Letters of Herman Melville* (New Haven: Yale University Press 1960), p. 280.
49. *Melville,* p. 330.
50. Underestimating the poet's fundamental and painstakingly developed differentiations, William B. Stein, *op. cit.,* pp. 233–34, stresses the affinity of Van Dyke, Veronese, and Rubens with their fellow painters because they all belong to "a sainthood of immoralists" and are "protagonists of the full life."
51. But how to speak o' the lamentable days
Hawsers parted, and started stays;
The
This, and the nine alternate readings that follow, are noted in the *Works,* vol. 16 (London: Constable & Co., Ltd. 1924). The many revisions made by Melville throughout his poetry belie Henry Chapin's statement, in *John Marr and Other Poems* (Princeton: Princeton University Press 1922), that "he did not set himself to master the poet's art."
52. Smiting there the metal
53. Helpless
54. Them the billows submerge
55. Dead they
56. From proneness on the
57. Unsurrendered colors
58. But, wherefore
59. Ah
60. War, with its dolorous days
Set
61. Shows (in Vincent and in the original galley proof).
62. This is Norman E. Jarrard's reading in *Poems by Herman Melville: A Critical Edition of the Published Verse* (Austin, U. of Texas, 1960). Other published versions are Lumbago, Lon Lumbago, and Long Lumbago.
63. Yes, Nature she (noted in the *Works*)
64. A scout
This, and the eight alternate readings that follow, are in the original edition of *Battle-Pieces* and in the 1924 *Works*. The version used in the present text is based on Melville's revisions in his copy of the book.
65. Lonesome
66. "In one of Kilpatrick's earlier cavalry fights near Aldie, a Colonel who, being under arrest, had been temporarily deprived of his

sword, nevertheless, unarmed, insisted upon charging at the head of
his men, which he did, and the onset proved victorious." (Melville's
note)

67. A strange lone land
68. They leave the road
69. We thought
70. They skirt the pool
71. "Certain of Mosby's followers, on the charge of being unlicensed
    foragers or fighters, being hung by order of a Union cavalry com-
    mander, the Partisan promptly retaliated in the woods. In turn, this
    also was retaliated, it is said. To what extent such deplorable pro-
    ceedings were carried, it is not easy to learn." (Melville's note)
72. My bluebirds
73. One's buttons shine
74. To come lone and lost
75. Bumped, in Vincent's edition, is a serious typographical error, since
    this is the line which reveals the slave-disguise of Mosby's hump-
    backed follower.
76. This defiant motto is omitted by Vincent.
77. Then (Vincent).
78. Swear (*Works*). Although Kaplan, in his *Battle-Pieces* facsimile,
    pp. xxii–iii, rightly criticizes Vincent for his many typographical
    errors, it should also be pointed out that Vincent admirably cor-
    rected many egregious errors in the 1924 *Works* as far as "Marquis
    de Grandvin" is concerned. Some of the footnotes which follow
    attest to this. In the case of obvious misspellings, where no ambi-
    guity of interpretation is possible, Vincent's corrections have been
    incorporated without annotation.
79. Parentheses omitted (*Works*).
80. Modernize even (*Works*).
81. With promise (*Works*).
82. Resigns (*Works*).
83. Thy charms (*Works*).
84. Undisguisedly (*Works*).
85. Of (Vincent).
86. Those (*Works*).
87. Ruddied (*Works*).
88. Flattered (*Works*). A third, and perhaps more appropriate read-
    ing, would be "flustered."
89. Both the *Works* and Vincent give Veronese the feminine name of
    Paola.
90. Hits (Vincent).

91. I daub, but daub it true (Vincent). With the additional comma "but" means "merely," which fits both the line that follows and Veronese's attitude toward his "off-hand sketch." Without the comma the statement becomes a boast.

92. Material (*Works*). This is a particularly misleading error, since it follows such terms as "Utility" and "huckster's street."

93. Bold (*Works*).

94. And so the noble Frenchman takes French leave, a genial, judicious way (*Works*).

95. "Whom they" is omitted in the *Works*.

96. Where you and yours (*Works*).

97. In the *Works* this is followed by two additional lines:
    With memories of an afternoon
    In Naples in the time of Bomba.
This may have been considered by Melville as an alternate conclusion. If "With" is eliminated, it becomes a more satisfactory ending than the one used in Vincent and in the present text.

98. A son (*Works*).

99. Each street (*Works*).

100. This line is omitted in the *Works*.

101. This (*Works*).

102. Here (*Works*).

103. Through (*Works*). Perhaps Melville's intention was to settle on one of these adjectives. "Thronged" is also in line 94, "streamed" in line 120.

104. Each girl (*Works*).

105. Nighs (*Works*).

106. My Rose (*Works*).

107. It drifted devious (*Works*).

108. Enwrought with flowers in gala day (*Works*).

109. In peak (*Works*).

110. "Pours" is omitted in the *Works*.

111. "Mooning in mind?" "Ah, lack-a-day!" (*Works*).

112. With jinglings (*Works*).

113. A peak (*Works*).

114. Abusing (*Works*).

115. On his feet (*Works*).

116. Tinkling low (*Works*).

117.   and when she
    Sat mutely passive, smiling still.
    For jest he took it?   (Vincent)

118. A balcony high (*Works*).

119. Here again, I stood (*Works*).
120. The earnest woman not ever wed (*Works*).
121. An odour (*Works*).
122. And her cry was this (*Works*).
123. The dark (*Works*).
124. So (*Works*).
125. Craftsman (both Vincent and *Works*). Within its context the plural form is called for.
126. "Paunched" is omitted in the *Works*.
127. Flanked (*Works*).
128. I heed (*Works*).
129. Spun (*Works*). The change to "he" indicates an avoidance of rhyme which would have blended the narrator's voice into the couplets that precede the boy's song and the series of rhymes (a real tour-de-force) that follow.
130. The sound (*Works*).
131. "Summing" is omitted in the *Works*.
132. Vincent begins Section VIII with line 634, and omits the introductory prose.
133. In a grandiose antic (*Works*).
134. The youngster (*Works*).
135. That bide (*Works*).
136. In white (*Works*).
137. The After-Piece is omitted in the *Works*.

SELECTED BIBLIOGRAPHY

Arvin, Newton. *Herman Melville.* New York: Sloane, 1950.

Bernstein, John. *Pacifism and Rebellion in the Writings of Herman Melville.* The Hague: Mouton, 1964.

Berthoff, Warner. *The Example of Melville.* Princeton: Princeton University Press, 1962.

————, ed. *Great Short Works of Herman Melville.* New York: Harper & Row, 1970.

Bezanson, Walter E., ed. *Clarel.* New York: Hendricks House, 1960.

Chapin, Henry, ed. *John Marr and Other Poems.* Princeton. Princeton University Press, 1922.

Chase, Richard V. *Herman Melville.* New York: Macmillan, 1949.

————, ed. *Melville: A Collection of Critical Essays.* Englewood Cliffs: Prentice-Hall, 1962.

Cohen, Hennig, ed. *The Battle-Pieces of Herman Melville.* New York: Thomas Yoseloff, 1963.

————, ed. *Selected Poems of Herman Melville.* Garden City: Doubleday, 1964.

Davis, Merrell R. and Gilman, William H., eds. *The Letters of Herman Melville.* New Haven: Yale University Press, 1960.

Fogle, Richard H. "Melville and the Civil War." *Tulane Studies in English,* IX (1959), 61–89.

————. "The Themes of Melville's Later Poetry." *Tulane Studies in English,* XI (1961), 65–86.

Hillway, Tyrus and Parker, Hershel, eds. *Directory of Melville Dissertations.* Evanston: Northwestern University, 1962.

Hillway, Tyrus. *Herman Melville.* New York: Twayne, 1963.

Howard, Leon. *Herman Melville.* Berkeley: University of California Press, 1951.

Jarrard, Norman E., ed. *Poems by Herman Melville: A Critical Edition of the Published Verse.* Austin: University of Texas, 1960.

Kaplan, Sidney, ed. *Battle-Pieces.* Gainesville: Scholars' Facsimile and Reprints, 1960.

Leyda, Jay. *The Portable Melville.* New York: Viking, 1952.

Mansfield, L. S. "Melville's Comic Articles on Zachary Taylor." *American Literature,* IX (1938), 411–418.

Matthiessen, F. O. *American Renaissance.* New York: Oxford University Press, 1941.

Melville, Herman. *Works,* Vol. 16. London: Constable, 1924.

Miller, James E. *A Reader's Guide to Herman Melville.* New York: Farrar, Straus and Cudahy, 1962.

Montague, Gene B. "Melville's Battle-Pieces." *University of Texas Studies in English,* XXXV (1956), 106-115.

Parrington, Vernon L. *Main Currents in American Thought,* Vol. 2. New York: Harcourt, Brace, 1930.

Plomer, William, ed. *Selected Poems of Herman Melville.* London: Hogarth, 1943.

Stein, William B. *The Poetry of Melville's Late Years.* Albany: State University of New York Press, 1970.

Vincent, Howard P., ed. *Collected Poems of Herman Melville.* Chicago: Packard, 1947.

Warren, Robert P., ed. *Selected Poems of Herman Melville.* New York: Random House, 1970.